A Child Alone

The Library of Holocaust Testimonies

Editors: Antony Polonsky, Martin Gilbert CBE, Aubrey Newman,
Raphael F. Scharf, Ben Helfgott

Under the auspices of the Yad Vashem Committee of the Board of
Deputies of British Jews and the Centre for Holocaust Studies,
University of Leicester

A Child Alone

MARTHA BLEND

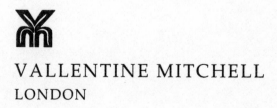

VALLENTINE MITCHELL
LONDON

First published in 1995 in Great Britain by
VALLENTINE MITCHELL & CO. LTD
Newbury House, 900 Eastern Avenue, London IG2 7HH

and in the United States of America by
VALLENTINE MITCHELL
c/o ISBS, 5804 N.E. Hassalo Street, Portland, Oregon 97213–3644

British Library Cataloguing in Publication data

Blend, Martha
    Child Alone. — (Library of Holocaust
    Testimonies)
    I. Title   II. Series
    940.5318092
ISBN 0-85303-297-1

A record of the Library of Congress Cataloging in Publication data
has been applied for

Typeset by Regent Typesetting, London
Printed by Watkiss Studios Ltd, Biggleswade, Bedfordshire

*To the memory of
my parents,
Elias and Paula Immerdauer,
and
my foster parents,
Annie and Will Greensztein*

*I wish to thank my husband
for his unfailing support
and encouragement in
the task of writing
this book*

Contents

List of Illustrations

The Library of Holocaust Testimonies

It is greatly to the credit of Frank Cass that this series of survivors' testimonies is being published in Britain. The need for such a series has long been apparent here, where many survivors made their homes.

Since the end of the war in 1945 the terrible events of the Nazi destruction of European Jewry have cast a pall over our time. Six million Jews were murdered within a short period; the few survivors have had to carry in their memories whatever remains of the knowledge of Jewish life in more than a dozen countries, in several thousand towns, in tens of thousands of villages, and in innumerable families. The precious gift of recollection has been the sole memorial for millions of people whose lives were suddenly and brutally cut off.

For many years, individual survivors have published their testimonies. But many more have been reluctant to do so, often because they could not believe that they would find a publisher for their efforts.

In my own work over the past two decades, I have been approached by many survivors who had set down their memories in writing, but who did not know how to have them published. I realized what a considerable emotional strain the writing down of such hellish memories had been. I also realized, as I read many dozens of such accounts, how important each account was, in its own way, in recounting aspects of the story that had not been told before, and adding to our understanding of the wide range of human suffering, struggle and aspiration.

With so many people and so many places involved, including many hundreds of camps, it was inevitable that the historians and students of the Holocaust should find it difficult at times to grasp the scale and range of the events. The publication of memoirs is therefore an indispensable part of the extension of knowledge, and of public awareness of the crimes that had been committed against a whole people.

Martin Gilbert
Merton College
Oxford

1 • Flashback

It was the day of the medical inspection. I joined the stream of mothers that trickled across the asphalt playground and into the school. At the far end of the corridor a row of chairs was placed ready to receive us, and I caught a glimpse of the crisp nurse, the bustling headmistress and the wary crocodile of boys and girls. The cast was assembled and the well-rehearsed performance about to begin. Suddenly my attention was diverted by something completely different: from the hall came the sound of children's voices singing in unison. Where had I heard that tune before? I realised with a pang of recognition that it was at my own first school many years ago and many miles away in the city of Vienna. The words were:

Hänschen klein	(Little Hans
Ging allein	All alone
In die grosse Welt hinein.	Into the great big world has gone.)

My mind was drawn back irresistibly to the people who had made up my small world in those early years of my life, and to the place where I was born.

* * *

Vienna, in the 1930s, had not arrived in the modern world. Its tall apartment houses, with their ornate facades, cornices and cupolas where birds nested, owed more to earlier centuries. Vienna was a capital city, but a very different one from London. There were no railway arches, sooty brick walls or rusty ironmongery. Everything was outwardly neater and

1

prettier, inside more harsh and primitive if you happened to be without wealth or servants. The centre was a framework for Imperial splendours: the great open squares, the tall St. Stephen's Cathedral, the baroque Opera House, the elegant shops and the restaurants that wafted the scent of coffee and pastries made with cream into the noses of passers-by. All the grown-ups had stories to tell about the Emperor, so that as a child I could well imagine a grand cavalcade sweeping down the Ringstrasse. It never happened while I was there – the Emperor was long exiled and all that glory departed – but in the people's imagination he lived on, and to this day, when I hear the Emperor Concerto, I feel a stirring of that old romanticism.

My parents rented a flat in the fifth district and this was my home for the nine years that I lived in Vienna. We had very few mod-cons: my mother did her washing on an old-fashioned board, and we ground our coffee by hand in a mill with a glass window. Our stove, a closed one on the Continental model, had a door into which you fed the fuel and a pipe that passed the smoke through an outlet in the ceiling. My mother had a gas cooker and a gas iron, but that was all. The people downstairs, more up-to-date than we were, boasted a radio, and from time to time, mechanical toys or gimmicks came my way. These often bore the legend 'Made in England', and when I was able to read the letters I would nag my parents to tell me what 'mahde in Anglund', as I pronounced it, meant.

Occasionally the twentieth century would make a modest intrusion into our lives, and we would go to the cinema. One of these outings to see a Shirley Temple film was marred by my urgent desire to go to the (inaccessible) lavatory. At other times when I passed one of these cinemas I would be intrigued by the outside of the building which gave little idea of the marvels within. But my parents still thought of the proper entertainment as the Opera. In his more exuberant moments, my father whistled 'La Donna e mobile' and my mother, who was a good storyteller, entertained me when I was ill in bed with the plot of *La Bohème*.

For a long time I thought that my interest in history and geography was fortuitous; but when I look back into my childhood, I realise how much of this I owe to my father's influence. He knew little of science and mechanics, but he loved to tell me the stories of the buildings we saw on our Sunday walks, and ask me the names of the countries of Europe and their capitals, some of which he had been to. Then there would be discussions about which countries were kingdoms, which were republics, which were empires. Empires were big countries.

'Then Austria is a big country and England, a little one?'

At this point my father would smile wryly and explain that it didn't always work out like that.

My father had had an education with a commercial bias and had worked as a book-keeper with a Viennese firm. He seems to have been reasonably prosperous as a young man – I have pictures of him looking handsome and elegantly dressed in the style of the 1920s. But the depression of the 1930s had its effect on us as on many families, and by the time I was approaching school age, we were living in straitened circumstances.

We never went short of food or essential clothing. My mother was a very good cook and could make *Gulasch*, *Wiener Schnitzel*, apricot dumplings and other tasty dishes. She also made a delicious jam known curiously as *'marmelade'*, and on my birthday she would conjure up a chocolate-cake decorated with silver balls and oozy bonbons called *pralinés*. But she became a great hunter of bargains in markets and would search assiduously for remnants for my clothes.

Our furniture was something between the massive, highly ornate pieces of the older generation and the spare lines of the 1930s – a simplified version of the former, still solid and respectable and adorned with a multitude of embroidered cloths and doyleys of all shapes and sizes. These were my mother's work. She had been brought up to this style of domesticity and her linen chest was full of sheets, tablecloths and petticoats, all decorated with the neat drawn-thread work on which she must have lavished a great deal of time.

Despite, or perhaps because of, this decorous equipment, I remember few things being replaced or bought afresh. My mother wore the same shabby dark blue coat year after year and the only holidays I remember were odd days by the Danube or a rare weekend in the country. From abroad, too, came rumblings of disaster: Wall Street had crashed, and an uncle of mine who had emigrated to America was reputed to have lost all his money. He died soon afterwards, leaving a widow and two children, but these blows only made a faint impression on the cocoon of my childhood.

My parents had not been born in Vienna as I was. Their families had lived in different parts of Poland, my father's in the Ukraine and my mother's near the Czechoslovak border. They were both Jewish, but had found the world of the Polish ghetto too small for them and had gone west to seek a new way of life. I don't know what the lure of Vienna was – certainly it proved no El Dorado of opportunity, but other people of similar origins had made a success of life there, and I suppose it held out some prospects lacking in my parents' home town. They had chosen to settle, not in the Jewish Quarter of Vienna, but in a mixed community.

In some ways my early childhood was a happy one: my mother devoted herself to looking after me and giving me a stable routine, and her good relations with acquaintances and neighbours surrounded me with warmth and friendliness. Nevertheless, there was an indefinable something lacking in my life. My parents had little formal social life, although from time to time friends and neighbours did drop in. It was the times between these visits that heightened my sense of loneliness and isolation. For my parents it may have been different: having both come from large families, the privacy of their life may have been a boon, but I, an only child, often longed for a new face and lively company.

I have said we lived in a mixed community: the mixture reflected the composition of the Austrian Empire, the ingredients consisting of Czechs, Poles, Hungarians, Austrians and Jews from any of these countries. The flat to the right of us was occupied by an elderly lady with a Czech name. I never saw her speak to anyone or have visitors. She evidently had a passion for geraniums, for her sitting-room window was almost obscured by a row of them in pots, climbing upwards and hiding the light. Every day I saw her bending over these plants to water them with a massive iron kettle. To me, she was a frightening figure, tall and obese, and when I passed her in the corridor, she would emit little sighing breaths that seemed to come from all over her body like steam from a leaky pressure cooker.

In the flat below us lived a Czech couple. The man looked rather sinister with a black eye-patch, but he had a son who was my first playmate. His mother encouraged the association at the time because it was said I 'spoke nicely' (that is, I didn't leave off the endings of my words as in the Viennese dialect). On Sundays, when I went there to tea, the man would prop his violin under his chin and his wife would pluck her zither with a metal thimble. It made the vibrant, twanging sound the world was later to associate with Harry Lime in the film *The Third Man*.

Upstairs was an oldish man, a bachelor who lived by himself. His passion was for herbs which lived in glass jars on shelves and on the tops of cupboards. Their several scents, sweet, harsh and aromatic, made me feel quite overcome on the rare occasions when I crossed his threshold with some message. This old man had a lady-friend who came to visit him and exchange favourite nostrums. I remember the meaning smiles of the grown-ups at this late-flowering romance. It was a relationship that gave amusement to the onlookers and innocent enjoyment to the old couple, an enjoyment that was later to be rudely terminated.

To the left of us lived a Hungarian widow and her daughter. I seldom saw the widow, but her daughter, who was young and vivacious, sometimes spent the evening with us. She and my father would reminisce about Hungary where my father had lived for a time, and I always longed for her to come again. Perhaps she sensed my mute appeal for her company, for she took me once to the Vienna Zoo where I embarrassed her with anatomical questions about some of the animals; but for me the outing was a complete success, something to look back on for weeks in a glow of pleasure.

One more family I remember vividly: a Jewish couple with two darkly attractive daughters who lived on the ground floor. The younger of these had not yet been admitted to the grown-up world and so found time to spare for me, whom she treated rather like a younger sister. She would make me shut my eyes to admire my long eyelashes, push a kink into my dead straight hair, tease me and swop giggly stories about the grown-ups. It was the elder sister, though, who really fascinated me: this paragon had boyfriends, stayed at hotels and went on skiing holidays in the mountains. I had never seen a mountain, much less skied on one, and I used to run my fingers down her Alpenstock in secret, hoping that some of this magic would rub off onto me.

Life in this little community went on in humdrum fashion punctuated by some minor excitements. My mother's younger sister got married and I have dim memories of a gypsy band playing the czardas at a restaurant where the reception was held. My father's sister and her husband decided to emigrate to Palestine and came to see us en route. My mother's sister-in-law in Belgium had a child who got his foot caught in a lift, with some resultant injury. She came to Vienna in search of a good surgeon and brought me a doll which I still cherish. Once, my father's niece from Budapest sailed down the river to pay us a visit, bringing me a present which I have never forgotten: a coral silk blouse and brown pleated skirt which fitted perfectly, to my great delight. The skirts my mother made me were usually too long on the assumption that I would grow into them. I wanted them to fit NOW and there were long arguments, with me refusing to wear them and my mother reluctantly taking them up a few centimetres. I remember these clothes better than the cousin who brought them – a childish narcissism I now have cause to regret.

At the age of four, I became interested in the printed page of the newspaper. I discovered that the shapes on the page represented letters which I could relate to familiar objects.

'What's the letter that looks like a swing?'

'That's M.'

'And the one that looks like half a loaf of bread?' (Viennese loaves were round.)

'That's a D.'

Once I knew the alphabet, I used to spell out the letters of a word, and my mother would put it together for me. One day, when we were out shopping, I asked: 'What's this word O-B-S-T?' and she replied that all I had to do was put the sounds together and they would make a word. I did so and found I had made the word *'Obst'* – German for 'fruit'. After this, I was able to read more and more by myself and later to devour story books with great pleasure.

My world of feeling at this time was largely a sensory one: getting into the bath was an agony of heat; having my nails cut left my fingers' ends vulnerable and made me shudder when I touched anything; winter gave me chilblains despite lace-up boots and gloves; summer brought scalding pavements and the sensual pleasure of taking off my shoes in a rough back alley, so that I felt momentarily at one with the barefoot children I secretly envied. The smell of the leather seats in a bus was so overpowering that I would be sick on the shortest journey, so it was easier for me to walk; paint was bubbly on old doors and could be punctured delightfully; shopwindows in the centre of town were deceptive: they curved inwards and you could lean into their concave depths; low walls were made to walk on and rails were good for swinging from.

The seasons were more sharply defined than in England: I remember autumn as a time of gathering darkness, pierced by the lurid glow of Hallowe'en. Then all the shops would be ablaze with dancing devils in brightest crimson. Their horrid tails stuck out from the watches in the local jeweller's window and their baleful faces glowered among the bracelets and rings. Next came Christmas and many weeks of snow and ice. With spring, the world changed perceptively: May brought delicate candles to the chestnuts, a vivid green to the trees in the Prater (Vienna's pleasure-garden) and lilac everywhere, white and mauve, spilling over old walls and in odd corners of shady walks.

My parents' religion, which was to play such an ominous part in my life, I can only reconstruct at this remove from their behaviour, as one estimates the size of a vehicle by the tracks it leaves in the snow. They had both had an orthodox Jewish upbringing, but had adapted their religion to the exigencies of modern life. The more obscure customs, about which I learned later, had long been discarded, as had strict adherence to the dietary laws. Although my mother drew the line at cooking pork or bacon, she bought her beef at a non-kosher butcher, which would have earned her the frowns of the strictly orthodox.

Yet my parents still celebrated the major festivals like Passover which occurs in March or April. Immediately before this, there would be an orgy of spring cleaning in which every cupboard was scrubbed clean. Then the special crockery used for Passover would be taken down from the attic. My mother would lay in a stock of eggs, almonds and matzos (unleavened bread). The almonds and egg-whites would be shaped into macaroons and the eggs whipped to make light, fatless sponge-cakes. On the first or Seder night of the festival my mother would place on the table the symbolic ingredients of the Seder: egg – a symbol of life – and salt-water and a shank-bone; also a mixture made from apples to represent the mortar used by the children of Israel when they laid bricks as slaves in Pharaoh's Egypt, and bitter herbs to remind the company of the hard times suffered by the children of Israel. There would be bottles of the sweet red Palestinian wines bought specially for the occasion, and a place set, as tradition demanded, for the prophet Elijah.

The celebration would begin when the first stars were out, with a blessing for wine and the recital of the story of the exodus from Egypt read in Hebrew from a book called the Hagadah. At intervals, the various symbolic foods would be passed round, accompanied by the drinking of wine and the eating of unleavened bread. This would be followed by a meal of soup with dumplings and chicken. At some point in the proceedings a piece of matzo would be hidden. It was the duty of the youngest member to look for it and claim a reward if they succeeded in finding it. The proceedings were wound up with the singing of traditional Hebrew hymns from the Hagadah.

We were quite a small party owing to the scattered nature of my parents' families – just ourselves and my mother's sister and her husband and later, her child. Nevertheless, these rituals were for me the highlight of an otherwise unexciting life. I was allowed to drink a little wine which made my cheeks feel flushed, and I felt very important when reciting the four questions – 'Why is this night different from all other nights?' and so on – traditionally asked by the youngest person who could read Hebrew.

My father retained a love of the Old Testament, and on winter evenings he would take down the big black Bible and read it to me. The stories of Genesis and Exodus stirred me immediately, though their impact was not so much moral as dramatic. I used to wait with bated breath to hear whether God would reprieve Isaac rather as one watches the train rushing towards the heroine strapped to the railway track; and when Joseph shamed his brother by revealing himself to them in Egypt, I wept hot tears of sympathy and dreamed of the day when I, who also felt misunderstood at times, would likewise shame my elders with my superior virtue and wisdom.

My father took me to the synagogue on the High Festivals of Rosh Hashanah, the Jewish New Year, which falls in the autumn, and Purim, when the story of Esther is recited, which falls in the spring. In the Purim service, I enjoyed joining in the racket made by the children with wooden rattles every time the name of the villain, Haman, was mentioned. At other times, I remember standing there, a diminutive figure in my best coat, waiting for the Scroll of the Law to be carried in triumph down our aisle so that I could touch a fringe of its ornaments and kiss it with my hand, as I had seen others do.

9

Sometimes I would look at my father and see tears at the corners of his eyes. This was puzzling to me, for in the ordinary way he never cried. I can only guess that he may have been reciting the prayer for the Dead – his own father having died while he was still very small. Or else the scene had struck some chord of emotion that I did not have the means to understand.

My mother never came with us at those times. Again, I am at a loss to know why. Perhaps she resented the subordinate role women play in the synagogue – they sit in a gallery apart from the men and take little part in the service – or perhaps she felt ill at ease with the wives of more orthodox or more prosperous men. Whatever the reason, it was always my father who took me to worship.

Next door to the synagogue was an annexe which housed the Religion School, and in this my mother did take an active interest. She introduced me to my teacher, settled me in, spoke to the other mothers and behaved much as she normally did. Of the reasons for my attendance I cannot be certain. My parents, as I have already explained, were not strictly observant, but I think they wanted me to have some knowledge of the tradition they were brought up in. It so happened that at this Religion School we learned little about the festivals that make up the Jewish calendar, but were taught instead modern Hebrew as a language. Whether there was a Zionist element in my parents' decision to send me there is something I can only speculate about. Whatever the motive, I liked my teacher, a pleasant young man with a brand new degree in Philosophy from Vienna University in addition to his Hebrew scholarship, and tried hard to learn the vocabulary and script of this new language. I still have the lines he made up for me inscribed into my autograph book:

Statt Französisch und Klavier	(French and piano
Rate ich, liebe Schülerin, dir:	Are all very fine,
Lerne deines Volkes Sprache	But don't let your study
und Geschichte,	Of Hebrew decline.)
Nur so manches verzichte.	

2 • A small world

From an early age I had been aware of being different from some of my neighbours and schoolmates. Christmas was just the same as any other day in my little family, but for my friend Grete it was a time of joy and excitement. The tree in her living-room festooned with coloured balls that tinkled melodiously, and the swags of tinsel, topped by a dazzling figure at its peak, had a glamour which nothing in my experience matched.

True, my mother lit candles on Friday night to celebrate the Sabbath and there was bread and wine on a snowy cloth. She waved her arms in a circular motion round the candles as, with head covered by a scarf, she recited the blessings for the Sabbath, thanking God for the duty of lighting the candles. On Simchas Torah, the celebration of the giving of the Law to Moses, we children were given nuts and small presents and I remember marching round the synagogue with a blue and white flag and later, reciting a poem in German from the pulpit. I felt very proud to have been asked to do this, but in my heart of hearts, though not for the world would I have hurt my parents by asking for one, I would have given quite a lot for a Christmas tree like Grete's.

There were other aspects of the Viennese scene which made a powerful and disturbing impression on my young consciousness, but I didn't know how to talk about them, so they remained buried in my mind. One morning a week the Christian children who made up the majority of the class had religious instruction. I was withdrawn from this, though I don't know who arranged for this – whether it was my parents' wish or whether it was taken for granted by the authorities that Jewish children did not stay for religious instruction. I never thought of questioning this and so, making my way out of the classroom at those times, I would meet the priest on his way into the school. I shuddered as I heard the squeak of his black shoes on the corridor and the swish of his soutane. He remained a sinister and frightening figure to me.

Near our flat was a convent. This was surrounded by a high wall and some of the windows facing the street had been bricked up. The building turned an altogether unwelcoming face to the outside world and this impression was not softened by the silent and shrouded figures of the nuns who crept in and out of this fortress without a backward glance. One thing puzzled me though: on some days the large gates would be open for a time and a shaft of bright sunlight would illuminate a segment of the courtyard. From inside this I could sometimes glimpse a child's swing and hear the sound of childish laughter. Was there a nursery school run by the nuns behind the high walls? At any rate, I could make no sense of these contradictory impressions.

Occasionally hearses passed in the street pulled by black-plumed horses, and a black-edged notice would appear on the street-door of a neighbouring apartment-block. When I asked my mother what this was for, she explained that it meant someone of the Catholic religion had died in one of the flats. Another strange thing I noticed was that my friend Grete had two celebrations a year: her birthday and her Saint's day, but I had only my birthday. Yet I remember my mother's insistence 'Du bist eine Wienerin' – 'You are Viennese.' Certainly I was born there and spoke the German language, but did this make me Viennese?

My very first friends happened to be boys, as there were no girls of my age in our flats. There was the boy downstairs, Karl, whose father wore the black eyepatch, probably to hide an old war wound, and Walter, who lived upstairs. Sometimes I played ball-games with them in the central courtyard of our flats, or more often indoor games like Ludo or dominoes in the cold Austrian winter. Walter's mother had fallen ill with a disease the grown-ups called '*Krebs*' – cancer. After an operation, presumably a mastectomy, she seemed well and cheerful for a time, but this remission did not last and she later took to her bed. My mother used to disappear upstairs several times a week to chat or read to her during her last illness.

Our daily routine before I went to school was unexciting: I watched my mother cook and bake, went shopping with her and was taken to the park to play or to visit her sister who lived in the twentieth district by the Danube canal. My mother's sister Dora was the only close relative who lived near and whom we saw regularly. I loved to visit my aunt Dora who gave me a lot of attention and allowed me to make dolls' clothes on her sewing-machine. When she told me that she was going to have a child of her own, I was fiercely jealous, but this feeling evaporated swiftly when I saw the baby, a helpless little thing with scars on its face from a forceps delivery. I kissed his tiny hand as a sign of acceptance and thought it a great treat in the coming months when I was allowed to push him in his pram in the rose-garden on the banks of the Danube canal where my aunt lived.

Other visits remain in my memory as less enjoyable. One such was to a remote cousin of my mother's who had a daughter with a crooked spine who wore a surgical jacket to correct this. She was a pretty little thing with blue eyes and curly golden-brown hair done in *Stoppellocken* – corkscrew curls. (My hair was dead straight, to my mother's chagrin.) However, I found the cage the little girl was wearing alarming and didn't know how to tell anyone so.

Another visit was to two elderly relatives of my mother's who lived among dark and gloomy furniture and spoke in quiet and solemn tones. I didn't find them very appealing, although my mother seemed to get pleasure from the visit. Still less congenial was a trip – never repeated – to the second district of Vienna where many Jews lived. We entered a house that seemed to be teeming with people: large women with funny-looking hair (orthodox Jewish women wear wigs over their close-cut hair) and bearded men in long black coats. My father and all the men I had so far come across were clean-shaven, so I had never encountered so many beards before. The purpose of this visit – there is no one I can ask about it – remains one of the many insoluble puzzles of my childhood.

Although my parents both came from large families, I knew hardly any of my other aunts and uncles personally. There were letters and occasional visits from some of them, but I never met either of my grandmothers. (Their husbands were long dead.) This seems strange now when trips to the other side of the world are commonplace, but poverty may have had something to do with it or the storm-clouds already gathering over Europe.

*   *   *

It would be hard for me to describe my mother as a person. I still carry a physical image of her in my mind, backed up by a photograph taken in 1939. Her name was Paula. She was a short, plump woman with a round, rosy-cheeked face and her hair pulled back into a bun. I remember feeling that this style was too severe and pulling some strands of her hair over her forehead to give a softer frame to her features. She looked matronly, although still in her thirties, and seemed to have neither the means nor the desire to dress fashionably. Another relative, who glided in and out of my life occasionally, cut a more elegant figure. I remember particularly a smart black cloak she wore and wished that my mother would emulate this attractive lady. My mother had small, well-shaped features and I remember her saying with a sigh, 'I was a pretty girl once'. This made me feel vaguely uneasy, as though I was the cause of her decline.

Of her character I know little except that she was what the Bible calls 'a virtuous woman'. She looked after my father and myself with unfailing assiduity, and was totally honest in her dealings and friendly with neighbours. She was quick-witted and good at languages. She spoke two Slavonic languages as well as German fluently, but probably had not had a great deal of formal education. She was, however, perceptive about people, judging by comments I remember her making. Occasionally, dropping her serious manner, she would mimic a pompous relative or acquaintance with deadly accuracy.

I was the kind of child who asked endless questions, which she did her best to answer. However, I guess that she was rather a reserved woman, quite unlike the ebullient stereotype of the Jewish mother exploding into exaggerated joy or fulsome praise or torrents of real or bogus sympathy. My mother and her sister spoke gently and quietly, but I suspect that she kept a lot of her feelings to herself. I wish fervently that she had told me about herself, her upbringing, her ideas. Of course I was very young and she could not have anticipated her death so soon, but with hindsight, if I were in that position, I would pour out all I knew to my child and not leave so much tantalisingly unrevealed.

My father was a tall, rather handsome man according to his photographs, although I remember him later as greying and careworn. All his brothers and sisters, so my aunt in Israel who is his youngest sister tells me, had the unusual combination of deep-set blue eyes and dark hair. His face, in contrast to my mother's, had a finely moulded bone-structure with high cheekbones, a pointed chin and prominent nose. My earliest memories of him are of being tossed up to the ceiling and other boisterous games. He was more outgoing than my mother and would laugh uproariously, on the few occasions we had visitors, at jokes and stories. My aunt describes him as *lustig* (lively) at the time she knew him. 'When he came into a room, the walls danced', as she put it, but I saw less of this side of him.

He was there only briefly in the evenings before my bed time during the week, but on Sundays he made up for this by taking me out, usually without my mother. I can only guess that she had had enough of my demands and needed some time to herself. My father, who saw less of me, gave me the impression that he enjoyed the times we spent together. He took me to the Prater, the Viennese pleasure-gardens with the big wheel made famous by the film *The Third Man*, a replica of which was put up in Blackpool. There were also walks to the Schönbrunn Palace near which was a building with classical columns set on a hill and surmounted by a huge eagle. I was greatly impressed by the size of this sculptured bird, symbol of a bygone power. It was called the Gloriette. Then there were walks to places of historical interest such as a wall in the Inner City on which hung a stone thrown by the Turks, a relic of the Turkish siege of Vienna which was broken by the bravery of Prince Eugen. We had learned a song about him at school. Sometimes there were trips up the Danube and on these we were joined by my mother.

As my parents had lost their first child, a boy who died soon after he was born, they were very proud of me and my rather precocious intelligence. As I have described, I had learned to read more or less by myself and my father taught me numbers, so that I was quite swift at counting and adding well before I went to school. My mother had a friend whose younger sister was one of the first women to go to Vienna University. I don't know whether she hoped I would do likewise, but certainly she took an uncommon interest in the education of a mere girl. I was encouraged to read, joined a library at the age of seven and my school reports were scrutinised, usually with pleasure, as I found learning easy and generally did well.

My father never criticised and seldom scolded me. It was left to my mother to dress me down when I had gone too far and to teach me table manners and the codes for saying 'hallo' and 'goodbye'. These were part of an elaborate ceremonial with gradations of formality. 'Adieu' was an ordinary goodbye, 'Grüss Gott' more formal and 'Ich küss die Hand' (usually shortened to "s die Hand') the most formal of all. This might be accompanied by a light kissing of the hand of the person you were saying goodbye to and a 'knickser', a curtsey from the knee. Vienna was a place where life was measured and ritualised.

I was very fond of both my parents, although I did feel bouts of anger against my mother sometimes, since it was she who disciplined and inevitably frustrated me at times. In my heart of hearts I had a guilty feeling that I loved my father the better of the two, but hoped earnestly that I did not betray this in any way.

After this loving but restricted circle, school was a welcome change for my restless temperament. Despite a rather abrupt beginning (there was no gradual introduction such as is common practice in England), I loved having things to do. The three Rs, singing and gymnastic exercises made up the curriculum, but I never found it dull. There was the added fascination of being with so many different children, some of whose names haunt me to this day: Faltynek (a Czech name) and Teufelholer (an unfortunate Austrian name – it means fetched by the devil). Our first teacher, Frau Gregory (strange that she had an English name), was a large, purple-faced woman, a dragon who insisted on instant obedience which she commanded with a loud rasp. However, I managed to keep out of trouble most of the time and so only once earned the ignominy of being sent into the corner for being slow to carry out some order. Our second teacher, Frau Leopoldine Hanner, was a slim woman in her thirties who spoke softly and encouragingly to us. I worshipped her and, for doing my best to please her, was rewarded by being chosen for the office of 'cupboard-monitress'. My job was to give out the workbooks for the class each morning.

In the hall, where there was a piano, we learned many songs: folksongs and songs by Schubert, 'Muss i' den zum Stätele raus', a song in the Viennese dialect, 'Heidenröslein' and 'Am Brunnen vor dem Tore'. These were some of the greatest treasures I took away with me from Austria. Many years later, I gasped with excited recognition when, as someone played a record of Schubert's 'Winterreise', I realised that the song-cycle contained one of my favourite childhood songs.

By now I was beginning to understand that there was a bigger world 'out there'. In the newspapers there were reports of a happening in a place called England. *Krönung* was the word that cropped up frequently, meaning 'coronation'.

'What is it about?' I asked my father.

17

'The king of England is going to be crowned.'

'Is our king going to be crowned too?' (I could never resist asking a supplementary.)

'No, we haven't got a king.'

'Why not?'

On and on went the questions until my father's patience gave out. I have dim memories of newspaper pictures of glamorous figures in long robes, crowns, tiaras and glass coaches – all the paraphernalia of a British Royal event.

* * *

Soon after this, I became aware of less pleasing news from 'out there'. 'Hitler' was now a name on everybody's tongue. Jewish people looked grim and tight-lipped when they spoke of him. I guessed he was not good news. I gathered he particularly disliked Jews. Why? I wondered. What had we done? Apart from feeling different because of my parents' religion, I had never encountered personal animosity. Neighbours, shopkeepers, teachers had all treated me in the same way as everyone else. My parents had few possessions anyone would envy, were law-abiding, had no personal enemies I knew of, so why did Hitler dislike us? I had no idea, nor did anyone explain this irrational hatred to me. Perhaps I would not have understood it if they had, but there seemed to be a change in the atmosphere which I could not help sensing, a darkening of the skies, inexplicable but ever-present and menacing to my childish perceptions.

I became more aware of the goings-on in the big world. The name 'Chamberlain' cropped up frequently, sometimes as a figure of hope, sometimes as a bungler. The name of 'Schuschnigg', the Austrian Chancellor, also swam into my consciousness. Now even my parents were talking regularly of political events and so were the grown-ups we met in the street. There was a feeling of pressure abroad as for an impending storm. I gathered that Austria was threatened with being taken over by its more powerful neighbour, Germany. Jewish people huddled together in anxious groups, while non-

Jewish acquaintances expressed pious hopes that such an annexation would not happen. I remember my friend Grete's mother lifting her hands skywards in a theatrical gesture of prayer to the 'Jewish God', as she put it, to save the country from such a fate.

On the radio my parents had recently acquired I now began to hear a harsh and strident voice screaming out hatred. It was the voice of Hitler. Then initials began to make a sinister impact: NSDAP – National Socialistische Deutsche Arbeiter-Partei, or National Socialist German Workers' Party, a harmless enough name, but why did people say the acronym 'Nazi' with such fear? Then there was 'Gestapo', an acronym of 'Geheime Staatspolizei' or secret state police. This name was pronounced with something like dread. It was all very disquieting. I heard of marches of Hitler-supporters in the centre of Vienna. My father went to one of these. He came back in apparently optimistic mood, insisting:

'Yes, there are a lot of them, but there are more of our people.'

My mother, who I think was unconvinced by his Micawberish view of the situation, sighed deeply.

Flags suddenly became important: there was the Austrian *Gruppenkreuz*, an ordinary cross, and the dreaded German *Hackenkreuz* or swastika, a menacing hooked cross in black in a white circle set into a red banner. In a surge of Austrian national feeling the *Gruppenkreuz* had been painted on pavements in the Inner City. This was to have dire consequences. Everywhere there was tension, argument, debate, yet nobody I knew moved at this point. Maybe, like my father, they thought the worst could not happen.

In that oppressive winter I had had my eighth birthday, rather different from the carefree celebrations of former years. True, my mother made the usual iced chocolate-cake with my name on it in silver balls, and a relative (I'm not sure how she was related) presented me with a *Stammbuch* (autograph-book). Her daughter, who describes herself as my cousin Mary Erster, started the contents off by writing a little verse in capital letters in rather tipsy lines (she had obviously only just learned to write). It asks me not to forget our friendship until the pug-dog speaks French. She or someone else had done a line-drawing of a little dog to illustrate this message, but I have no recollection of this young person and never saw her again. However, I still have the autograph-album, my most prized possession. It contains many well-intentioned exhortations to greater effort and unassailable moral truths – dinosaurs from a vanished world which was to be superseded by a brutal order that cared nothing for such delicate moral concepts. One page of this book I can never open without tears, as it contains verses written by my father, the only relic I have of him, apart from some photographs.

Soon after this, I had had a bout of childish illnesses: mumps, followed by measles, followed by whooping-cough. Dr Singer, our family doctor, noticed that I, who had been quite a plump, robust-looking child, had become thin and pale. He insisted on giving me a course of ultra-violet treatment for which, knowing my parents could not afford any more doctor's bills, he made no charge. I remember sitting on the red leather chairs of his smart waiting-room with some envy, as he seemed to be part of an altogether more affluent and privileged world. However, this privilege was not to last for much longer.

After my illness I returned to school, feeling shaky at first, but gradually regaining my strength. One morning I set out as usual, but was surprised to see some new flags being put up in front of the music-school I passed on my way. I was confused about what they were, but sensed that something strange was happening. The streets, normally full of hurrying school-children, were deserted. Was it a holiday? When I got to school, my classroom was silent and empty, save that at the far end stood my teacher, Frau Hanner, red-eyed and distressed. I had never seen her like this before and was gripped with a gnawing sense of foreboding. She was surprised to see me, but suggested, with gentle concern, that I drank the milk that was provided for us by the State before I went home. I gulped down my milk with a sickening feeling in my stomach and ran home as fast as I could.

There I discovered what had happened. We must have been the only people who didn't have their radio on that morning, and so my mother had sent me to school, unaware that Hitler's troops had marched into Austria, now said to be part of greater Germany. The *Anschluss* or joining-up of two countries had taken place.

LEBE GLÜCKLICH, LEBE FROH,

WIE DER MOPS IM PALETOT

UND VERGISZ DIE FREUNDSCHAFT NICHT

BIS DER MOPS FRANZÖSISCH SPRICHT.

DEINE KUSINE MARY ERSTER

2.I.1938.

Many years after Martha was given the autograph-album in which Mary Erster's poem was inscribed, she met by chance a Belgian refugee who was able to show her a list of Jewish deportees from Antwerp. The name of her mother's brother Mauritz Kramer was on it, with that of his wife, née Erster. Evidently Mary Erster was a kind of cousin after all.

3 • Living under the swastika

The dreaded event had become a reality and its impact was devastating. The Jews of our acquaintance were shocked and shaken. At this point the grown-ups no longer made the effort to conceal from me their consternation or the depressing news of despairing people who had committed suicide rather than face what, judging by his treatment of the Jews in Germany, Hitler had in mind for them. One such was the jeweller round the corner who, it was rumoured, had cut his throat and been found in a pool of blood. I had often admired the display in his window, never imagining what was to be his fate. So far I had been kept in the dark about the details of the tightening screw of Hitler's persecution of the Jews, but I sensed that dreadful things were in store to make someone take such an extreme remedy.

I remember a feeling of numbness that seemed to prevail for a little after this – at any rate among the Jewish people I knew. Living as we did, some distance away from the centre of the city, I was not aware as yet of the Nazi parades and celebrations that went on there. Nevertheless, some of this triumphalism did penetrate to the streets where we lived. Suddenly hoardings bristled with swastikas and men in brown shirts and with Nazi armbands appeared out of nowhere. Sometimes my mother would recognise a neighbour in one of these strutting figures as she stared at him in disbelief.

My parents had never been frequent cinemagoers and now they stopped going altogether, so I was not aware of the Nazi propaganda films of the time. However, I did somehow get hold of a copy of *Der Stürmer* magazine, which specialised in hideous caricatures of Jewish people. I looked at these revolting pictures of people with swollen bodies, faces twisted into horrible grimaces, and monstrous noses. Looking at myself in the mirror all I could see was a very ordinary little girl neither very tall nor very short for her age, with hazel eyes, small, straight features and light brown hair. Had these people who produced the magazine been looking in the kind of distorting mirror they had in Vienna's pleasure-garden, the Prater? I did not understand that hate can create the same effect.

One evening, my father and I were sitting at the table and my mother was about to dish up the supper. The radio was on. Suddenly, my father pricked up his ears.

'Did you hear that? There's going to be a plebiscite!' he shouted to my mother who was coming out of the kitchen.

'What's a plebiscite?' I asked.

'The people are going to put on paper whether they want Austria to belong to Germany or not.'

'Then the people will say they don't want the Germans and they'll go away?'

Great was my disappointment when, weeks later, my father's newspaper gave the result as 99 per cent in favour of the *Anschluss*. Everybody suspected that the result was rigged, but there was little anyone could do about it. My father seemed to take some comfort from the number of people in the Austrian cities of Graz and Linz who had voted against the majority, but they made no difference to the outcome – Jews had not been allowed to vote at all, but even if they had been, they were too small a minority to affect the result.

Soon after this came the first reports of actual aggression: those unlucky Austrian crosses painted on the pavements in the centre of Vienna offended the new overlords. Their remedy was to get their young blackshirts to round up Jewish women and old Jewish men with beards and force them to kneel on the pavements and scrub out the unwelcome signs of Austrian nationalism. At the time I knew nothing about the jeers and brutality that accompanied this activity, or that they were forced to scour the pavements with a toothbrush and an acid that burnt their hands, but the mere fact that these people were dragged out of their homes and humiliated in this way for no reason made me cringe. My mother had been spared this particular ordeal. In fact, I didn't know anyone personally who had been made to participate in this public humiliation, but news of it spread to our district, adding to my bewilderment and insecurity.

After the shock of the *Anschluss* and the steady stream of propaganda against the Jews, I felt that I was caught in a web of tension and hostility not of my making, but from which I had no power to extricate myself. That I and my family had done nothing to deserve it made it all the more sinister.

In the street, wherever you went, there were uniformed men in brown or black shirts with swastika armbands stepping out aggressively in their jackboots. Every week we were importuned by people shaking their collection-boxes in our faces for this or that Nazi cause. Army lorries packed with fierce-looking blackshirts sent out threatening signals as they swept past. At other times, the snarl would turn into a smile: the lorries would be laden with gifts to the Austrian people from a beneficent Führer. A burly SS-man would stand astride the tailboard, smirking ingratiatingly as he held out bananas for the taking. I knew instinctively that these goodies were not intended for me and kept my hands tightly clenched as I crept away from the happy throng.

On my way home, I wondered how it was that neighbours who had until recently been friendly, now kept their distance, and acquaintances who a short while ago had trumpeted their devotion to Austria now seemed comfortable with the new order. One day I could hardly believe my ears: from the flat below came the unmistakable sounds of *'Heute haben wir Deutschland'* – today we have Germany, tomorrow the world – the proud boast of the Nazi Party. My friend Karl was thumping out the tune on his piano with gusto.

There were other unpleasant songs denigrating my people, one of which went

> *Ein Volk, ein Reich, ein Führer*
> *Schuschnigg wird immer dürer,*
> *Die Juden immer fetter.*
> *Heil Hitler unser Retter.*

The first line is part of the Nazi slogan 'one people, one state, one leader'; the second line refers to the former Austrian Chancellor who for some reason is supposed to be getting thinner and the next line says that the Jews are getting fatter. Quite untrue, this; we were certainly not thriving. What was true was that what with the flags and banners, the aggressive parades and the shrill voices on the radio of Hitler, Goering and Goebbels it felt as though an orchestra was working up to a violent climax. What was likely to happen when these violent impulses were released against the Jews was becoming increasingly clear.

A few of them, reading correctly the signs of what had been happening in Germany, had had the foresight to leave. Among those was my father's youngest sister and her husband who emigrated to Palestine in 1933. But the majority, like my father, resisted the idea of pulling up such precarious roots as they had in Austria and travelling into the unknown. They put too much trust in the *Gemütlichkeit* (warmth) of the Austrian people – a sentiment which was to prove entirely bogus where they were concerned, as false as the Latin slogan promising justice on the Parliament building in Vienna. Now that the frontiers were closed, they were trapped. Daily the propaganda machine described them as unwelcome guests, nuisances, the cause of all Europe's troubles; yet they were forbidden to leave. And indeed, where could they have gone? No country was keen to have them. They would have given all they had to get to the United States, but the US had an immigration quota far smaller than the thousands who sought asylum. An affidavit to enter America was the open sesame to

25

survival, but these were like gold dust. Britain and all the other European countries also operated strict immigration quotas, so escape was an option only for the lucky few – the wealthy and the famous.

With the annexation of Czechoslovakia, German expansionism was no longer a boast but a threatening reality. Nowhere now seemed safe. Jewish people who had not managed to get away clung together for comfort. Our small flat, which had seen visitors only infrequently, now suddenly became a meeting-place for people I had never known before. Each visitor nourished a little flame of hope: one had an invention that might help him to get out; another had an uncle in Manchester or a cousin in China who might be prevailed upon to put up the large sum of money demanded by the Nazis for safe conduct. It was an irony that was lost on me at the time, but of which I am fully aware now, that the very people who were calling us avaricious were greedily extracting every *pfennig* they could from these unfortunates.

As all my father's acquaintances had lost their jobs by Nazi decree, they tried their hand at any work they could get to feed their families. My father did decorating jobs for neighbours. I still remember the sponges dipped in coloured distemper he used to make stipple patterns on their walls. Some men earned a little money by standing in queues at the American embassy for their wealthier brethren (this queueing could take days); some later shovelled snow in the cold winter of 1938–39 – anything to stave off hunger.

When his new source of income dried up, my father got a temporary job in a factory that bottled apple juice. I remember going to see him in the cool cellar where the juice was processed. There were machines that strained the liquid into dark bottles and a pervasive sour smell. Whenever someone opens a bottle of apple juice today I am transported back into that cellar, watching my father attend to those machines. What his thoughts were about being obliged to do such unskilled tasks I don't know, but he never complained. I suspect he was glad to do anything that would give us our daily bread.

When work became even more scarce for my father, my mother announced:

'Frau Kiwetz tells me the American Jews are setting up a soup-kitchen in Vienna. I thought I'd try it.'

'Charity?' said my father angrily.

Nevertheless, next day my mother put her pride in her pocket and we set off armed with a large screw-top jar to get whatever handout was available. When we reached the building where the food was being distributed, we were directed to a gloomy basement, where we queued up for what seemed hours. Eventually we got to some trestle tables. Here a soup made from vegetables and beans was dispensed from a huge metal pot into the jars and bottles of the people who had waited patiently for these meagre rations. In charge of operations was a large woman – the wife of a rabbi – who shouted orders in a harsh voice to the servers under her command. As she leaned her bulky form backwards with ladle poised, I shuddered at the pattern of red blotches that disfigured her face. My mother, on the other hand, seemed unperturbed as she chatted to the women nearest her in the queue. They turned out to be all sorts of distressed gentlefolk: a music teacher now bereft of pupils, the wife of a professor who had been dismissed from his post, a local dressmaker. All were reduced to accepting this form of relief.

Now came news of fresh harassment. My parents had tried to shield me from this, but I picked up a good deal from the conversations of neighbours. Some men had been rounded up by the dreaded SS and sent to places which struck terror into speaker and listener alike. They were called Dachau and Buchenwald, and after I heard fragments of whispered tales of what went on there, their very names sent shivers down my spine. One story struck me with particular horror: people had had word that their husband/father/son who had been perfectly healthy before he was taken away had died in custody and that if the relatives wanted his ashes they must put up a sum of money for the privilege.

About this time a measure was introduced which affected

me personally: a decree that Jewish children were not fit to be educated with Aryan children and must be taught in separate classes. Up to now my teacher had regarded me as a prize pupil, always ready to throw herself into any activity with enthusiasm. How did this square with the official view? I knew I hadn't changed, so this blanket condemnation was all the harder to bear. Suddenly I was cut off from the place which had been a safe haven, the teacher I loved and the children I had known, among them my friend Grete. I now had to enter the school building by a different door and found myself in a different classroom with a new teacher who was said to be Jewish. She was nice enough, but no substitute for my beloved Leopoldine Hanner. For the first time I was in a class with boys as well as girls. There was an air of impermanence about this arrangement – everybody was trying to get somewhere else – Switzerland, France, Sweden – anywhere out of the clutches of the Nazis. Our teacher, Fräulein Steckler, went through the motions of teaching us, but I don't remember learning much in that class, though I still have the exercise book I used. It contains little more than the words of the Lorelei song.

By now we were all living on a knife-edge of terror, expecting the worst at any moment and dreading the sound of heavy jackboots stomping up our stairs and the harsh voices of the SS ordering a much-loved husband, father, brother into their cruel custody. The intended victims had few options: they could hide, but where and for how long before they were discovered or betrayed? Resistance was impossible, as the stormtroopers were heavily armed and appeals were useless, for compassion was not in their vocabulary. They even resorted to the well-tried tactic of asking the children to reveal the whereabouts of their fathers. So my mother coached me:

'If they ask you where your father is, say you don't know. You will remember, won't you?'

'Oh, yes,' I replied fervently.

Against this background, formal learning at school was impossible. Nevertheless, we were encouraged to use our talents by drawing, reciting poetry and singing. One little boy I still remember: he was called Grünbaum. I can picture him now: thin and undersized with brown hair and eyes which had a look of deep sadness. From this unpromising frame came an amazingly full-throated and beautiful voice whose tones rang out with compelling richness in that doom-laden classroom. He sang a song which I later – many years later – discovered to be Schumann's *'Die beiden Grenadiere'*. It is about two soldiers bewailing the defeat of Napoleon and expressing their undying loyalty to him. Some parts of the tune echo snatches of the Marseillaise. The song had little to do with our situation, but he infused it with such a depth of melancholy, such unutterable sorrow that the memory of it haunts me to this day.

Fear and hate were now our constant companions. One went to sleep with them and woke up as from a nightmare – except that the nightmare remained during one's waking hours. My mother did her best to protect me, but the events which caused the troubled look on her face were all too obvious. One bright spot was the unexpected kindness of a neighbour – the husband of the woman my mother had befriended when she was ill. He, a chef at a Viennese hotel, used to leave us *Punschkrämpfl* – pastries rather like Genoese fancies – on the window-sill outside our flat. That was as far as he felt he could go in support of our beleaguered family.

I saw no more now of my old friend Grete, but made some new friends, both called Ruth. Ruth Gartner was in my class at school and lived round the corner to me. She had a pretty bedroom full of pictures of Shirley Temple displaying her dimples and curls and a dolls' house with a battery that gave real light, which served as the focus for our play. Another friend, Ruth Ashkenaze, was the daughter of someone my mother had met in the queue for soup. Her father had been a professor, but, like all Jewish professionals, had been dismissed from his post. I used to visit Ruth in her spacious flat. She was a charming little girl with a small pointed face, bright eyes and heavy brown braids that seemed much more impressive than my short straight bob. Her mother put salt on the tomatoes we had for tea, a new flavour I can still remember tasting for the first time. We played dominoes and board-games as we had done in happier times.

Another distraction was the *Turnverein* or gymclub. We had a neighbour called Mr Boritz whom I liked because he always had a smile and a kind word for me. His daughter, Adi, ran a Zionist club for children. I didn't actually learn much about Zionism there, but I enjoyed the exercises of various kinds which gave some outlet for my energies. There were bars to swing from – something I loved to do, and horses to vault over.

At about this time, my mother decided it would be a good idea for me to learn English, so she took me along to our synagogue. There she enrolled me in a class of adults who were learning it in preparation for emigrating to the English-speaking world. I don't remember what reason she gave me for this scheme, but it must have been a convincing one to make me stay in that class. I was the only child there. The teacher was a thin young woman with an Italianate face and a brisk manner. She looked at me doubtfully as my mother led me in. 'Sit there and pay attention!' she ordered.

Her lesson began with the basics – the verb 'to be' written up on the board, which we all had to learn, and then she took us through some more verbs and the names of objects round the room. Pointing to it, she said:

'That's a window. What is it?'

'A window', we chorused dutifully.

After a few of these lessons we were asked to write a composition in English – I forget on what subject – but I did my best with the meagre resources at my disposal, duly handing it in. All the students had their essays returned the following week with comments. On mine she had written 'All things considered, on the whole, not too bad.'

Stung by this faint praise, I resolved that I would show this woman what I could do. She might well have been surprised to hear me speaking fluent English two years later.

The next outside event, however, was to have fearful consequences for my family, banishing all possibility of normal living. A young Jew named Grünszpan, outraged by the Nazis' cruel treatment of his parents, had shot dead a Nazi official. The reprisals were massive and indiscriminate. That night in the autumn of 1938 which became known as *Kristallnacht*, Jewish shops were smashed and looted, religious old men with beards were beaten up and, in every town and city, synagogues were burned. The worst was yet to come, for that night the jackboots did come stomping up our stairs, taking my father with them. My mother, despite her pleas, was as powerless to prevent this as I was. Where he was being taken and whether he would ever return I had no idea. Next morning at school I discovered that many other pupils' fathers had been taken away. In our usually orderly classroom there were bouts of hysterical laughter, excited discussions and quiet sobbing.

Some days later my father did return. What torment he must have gone through while he was away or where he had been sent he didn't let on to me, no doubt to save me further suffering. I only found out about the treatment he must have had by reading accounts of survivors many years later. He showed no obvious physical signs of abuse, but his jaunty stride and quizzical smile were gone.

The stormtroopers had not spared the old man upstairs either. He was dragged away, insisting that he was not Jewish and had a certificate of baptism to prove it, but this conversion cut no ice with the Nazis who ignored his protests. Where his Aryan lady-friend was at this time nobody knew, but the old man was not seen in our flats again.

I remember my parents conferring anxiously about possible means of escape. One idea was to appeal to my father's sister in Israel for the sum of money required to leave the country. Another possibility was for my mother to come to England as a domestic servant, taking me with her. Many women saved their lives in this way, working as maids in hotels and private homes. Unfortunately, my mother rejected this idea, not out of pride but because it would have meant leaving my father whose chances of getting away were slimmer with each menacing week. One more option remained: my mother had been in touch with our family doctor and he had told her of an organisation which I later discovered was called 'Kinder-transport'. This was a scheme for bringing unaccompanied children out of Germany, Austria and Czechoslovakia to live in hostels and foster homes in England. Our Dr Singer had given my mother the address of a London couple who were willing to foster a child, and my parents set in motion the machinery that was to take me to England in a few months' time.

When my parents broke this news to me, I was devastated and burst into hysterical sobs at the mere thought. After all, I was an only child – the apple of their eye – and had never been parted from them before. How could I leave them now? Then the persuasion began: it was to be a holiday – just a year apart and we would all be reunited in Palestine. A year in itself is an eternity to a nine-year-old and, with the turn events were taking, the possibility of a reunion in Palestine seemed as remote as one in Paradise. There was little joy for me then in those reassuring words, but I realised that my protests were useless. My parents' minds were made up.

I felt as though some force far stronger than myself was dragging me to an abyss and I had no power to prevent it. Although I was still very young, I had seen and understood the build-up of terror in the last two years, so I knew very well that my parents were doing this out of sheer necessity. Nor did I feel that they were rejecting or punishing me. True, I could not have imagined the precise means the Nazis would have used to bring about my destruction had I stayed, yet I had a feeling of foreboding that some dreadful catastrophe was about to overtake us. This was daily strengthened by the aggressive propaganda against us and the mounting restrictions on the most basic activities of life, as well as the constant threats to our safety. There was no mistaking my parents' motives in wanting to get me out of this, yet that the rescue should take this horrifying form was like a death to me. The best I could do was to put it out of my mind as much as possible.

Meanwhile my father was again out of a job. My mother, intelligent though she was, had no formal qualifications for working outside the home. Nevertheless, to ease our desperate financial situation, she took on a job as companion to an old lady. She mostly carried out her duties while I was at school, but once or twice for some reason she took me with her to the lady's flat. I saw her minister to her charge, wash her, comb her hair, prepare a meal for her on a tray. This came as a complete revelation to me. I had never thought of my mother as belonging to anyone but me and to see her looking after someone else with the solicitude I had thought was reserved for myself came as a shock. I found the relish with which she apparently did this disgusting. In fact, I thought she was really overdoing it when flattering remarks about the lady's thin white hair, which looked repellent to me, were added as an extra flourish to the service. Looking back on this scene, I realise now that, as an only child used to being the centre of my mother's attention, I resented strongly the discovery that she could switch her talents onto another object with such ease. It never occurred to me that my upbringing had been unusual in that I had enjoyed her undivided attention for so long.

During the period my mother worked she must have earned a fairly reasonable salary. We could afford no luxuries, but she did buy herself a smart new winter coat and hat for the first time in several years. For me she bought a camel-coloured double-breasted coat with a conical red hat. Her employers must have been wealthy, to judge from the thick carpets and expensive brocade curtains and soft furnishings in their flat. One day my mother came home white-faced: she told us that she had found a large wad of missing bank notes which had slipped behind a sofa. Being honest by nature, my mother had handed it to her employers, hoping that her virtue would be rewarded by some modest share in the find. To her disappointment, she was only thanked in words. Had she, I wonder, been weighing up in her mind the sum that would buy our freedom? Did she regret her impulsive honesty? I shall never know the answer to these questions, for she told me no more than the bare facts, so I can only speculate.

Around this time, my interrupted English lessons were resumed. There was now a compelling reason for this. My mother had found another acquaintance whose daughter was waiting to emigrate to the USA. She had lost her job and was only too willing to fill up the time by teaching me gratis. She was a slim, elegant young lady with a fashionable bobbed hairstyle and painted fingernails. She had a good working knowledge of English, some of which she imparted to me by means of a little book called 'A Hundred Very Short Stories'. The tales were mostly humorous anecdotes. One of them was about a mistake over an order for a consignment of monkeys: the order was for four or five and the delivery was of 405 'grinning apes' – I remember the very phrase. The book also had in it the rhyme

> There was a little girl
> And she had a little curl
> Right in the middle of her forehead.

I was fascinated by this verse and rolled it round my tongue with a strong guttural accent. I learned quite a lot of useful vocabulary in this way.

While I was having my lessons in my teacher's flat, I would hear a loud banging noise coming from the floor above. When I asked what the cause of this was, I was told that the people in the flat above (*echt* Aryan) were soon going to take over the one below them which belonged to my teacher's family and were constructing an internal spiral staircase to join the two flats. There was nothing the present occupants could do except put up with the noise and disruption, as Jews had no right to complain. Compared with the suffering of poorer people with no hope of escape, this was a minor hardship, but to me those blows on the ceiling were potent symbols of an irrational order that could blast into your life unbidden and devastate it without redress.

In the spring of 1939 my mother's sister had a second baby – an ill-timed birth if ever there was one. I was taken to see my aunt during her lying-in and was allowed to see the new baby after the midwife had finished attending to the mother. He was a beautiful boy. In the coming weeks I was again allowed to wheel the new baby as I had wheeled his brother, now four years old, in the rose garden near the Brigittenauerlande where my aunt lived. I enjoyed playing with him, tickling his toes and blowing on his tummy. I still have the pictures of both children in my album: the older boy dressed up in a Lord Fauntleroy suit borrowed for the occasion and the new baby, by now a chubby six months old, looking up from a rug with large wondering eyes. My mother sent me their pictures after I had arrived in England.

All this time the screw against us was being tightened. A decree came out that Jews were not allowed to sit on park-benches, use sport facilities or go to places of entertainment. The Hitler salute – 'Heil Hitler' shouted with upraised arm – was obligatory in all public buildings. Virtually everyone who was not Jewish had taken to wearing a swastika badge on their lapel. What had happened to bring about such a change in the behaviour of people I had known for years was hard to fathom. I felt more than ever excluded and discriminated against. Sometimes I would fantasise that I was an Aryan child like the others, able to wear the desirable badge and lead a normal life. At other times, I would have dreams of revenge when I would imagine the tables turned, with the Jews in power and the Nazis as victims. I would think up some choice punishments for my tormentors, but the reality was very different. We were a small, unarmed, ill-prepared minority and the rest of the world ignored our plight.

In previous months my father had tried to cheer us up with parables. He would say:

'The Jews are like ink and the Nazis like water. Add ink to water and the water turns black; add water to ink and it's still inky.'

I don't know that I was totally convinced by this idea. Did he mean we would survive, despite the threats against our very lives?

Another time he said: 'You can't see it, but the foreign press is photographing all that's going on here. They have cameras concealed in their buttonholes.'

That may have been so, but for all the help the outside world gave us, we might as well have been living on the moon.

4 • Little refugee

In the spring of 1939, about a year after the *Anschluss*, letters began arriving from the couple who were offering to foster me in England. They enclosed a photograph of themselves – both short people – he in winter coat and trilby hat and she a rather dumpy figure in fur coat and halo hat. Both looked benign and eminently respectable – wealthy even. This fuelled my mother's propaganda: 'You see, you're going to have a good time with kind people.'

Kind they certainly seemed to be, for they expressed great sympathy for my parents' plight and assured them that they would take good care of me. I'm certain that the decision to send me away was as painful for my parents as for me, but there must have been some crumb of comfort for them from these reassuring letters. My mother was loud in her praises for these wonderful people who not only showed compassion, but were prepared to give such practical help. My mother was not given to hyperbole, so I was surprised to hear her say:

'I would go into the fire for such people.'

This seemed excessive to me who was trying hard to pretend the whole thing was never going to happen.

* * *

I felt that I was living in a world that was remorselessly crashing around my ears and would plunge me into a pit from which there was no escape. Yet elsewhere wheels were turning to provide me with that last chance of flight: an official letter came ordering me to attend at a clinic for a medical inspection. When my mother and I arrived there, she was told to wait outside while I was taken to another room where there were

37

several other girls. There was quite a spread of ages, the youngest eight- and nine-year-olds like me, the oldest well into their teens. We were brusquely ordered to strip to the waist for our examination. For children like me that was no great matter, but for the teenagers who had already developed breasts and wore brassières it was an obvious embarrassment to have to stand there stripped in a line of many girls. It was a new experience for me too. I knew women had breasts and wore brassières, but it was a shock to see girls only a few years older than myself with miniature versions of this equipment. However, in this as in all other dealings with us, respect for modesty and sensitivity were not on the menu. You did as you were told, or else.... After a brief examination of my mouth and chest, I was allowed to get dressed and go back to my mother. The message of that day was that the separation I was trying to shut out of my mind was coming ever closer.

Books were the only means of escape from this fearful reality, so I read avidly whatever I could get hold of from the library or the shelves of friends. At this point, my parents seemed to be too distracted to supervise my reading, so anything was allowed. One book I remember was a collection of stories about the Jewish community in Poland which featured a monster called the Golem – a non-human creature a bit like Frankenstein, who seemed to mess up everything he was supposed to do. I found the whole idea frightening, not least because my own life was in such a mess. A completely different book was a romantic story about a war-wounded young man who won the love of a charming young woman despite his disabilities. I warmed to this theme, but could find no echo of its delicate sensibility in the world around me.

Meanwhile the Jewish community in Vienna was abuzz with rumour, speculation, debate. Hope and despair alternated in bewildering succession: one day there were stories of horrors – people had been rounded up, forced to dig their own graves and shot; at other times there were tales of the humanity of an SS man who had permitted some small concession. It was a cat-and-mouse game that the Nazis played with evident relish.

The prevailing atmosphere also had this two-edged quality: on the one hand, aggressive struttings and chants; on the other, the wistful sentimentality of songs such as '*Schön ist die Jugend, ja – sie kommt nicht mehr*' (Youth is beautiful, but it doesn't come again).

The rumour that was rife in the early part of that summer was that people were going to be deported to the Austrian border. In ordinary circumstances, such a scheme would have seemed outrageous, but these were not ordinary circumstances and it was well understood by the Jews of Austria that whatever slender claim they had had to basic human rights in the past certainly did not apply now. Any move, some thought naively, would be better than staying where they were to face ever-increasing persecution. But which border? My parents had taken it into their heads to think that they might be sent to the Hungarian border. My father had relatives in Budapest – three nieces – and if we could only get into Hungary, we might yet have a chance of leading a more normal life there. In anticipation of this, my mother sent by post a parcel of her best linen. It contained tablecloths and pillowcases with drawn-thread work, embroidered chairbacks and cross stitched cushion-covers as well as underslips with appliquéd hems – all my mother's handiwork. A futile gesture, but perhaps for my mother at this time some action, however inappropriate, was better than none. Maybe it gave some temporary satisfaction to the squirrel-instinct for hiding away treasures that many women have. Whether these items ever reached their destination and what happened to them after that I have no idea.

The next event in my life is so bizarre and horrific that I have to pinch myself to convince myself that it really happened: once more the jackboots mounted our stairs to take away my father. He was unarmed, so resistance against these heavily armed young thugs would have been useless. My mother, who was distraught with worry about his fate, somehow found out that he had been taken to a certain police-station and that he was going to be deported. Where to, nobody would say exactly. For some reason which I cannot fathom, my mother had persuaded herself that he would be sent to Hungary. Wishful thinking perhaps. What followed sounds totally irrational, but rationality had long disappeared from the scheme of things in Vienna. As far as I know and can remember, my mother pleaded with the authorities to deport us to Hungary too and believed that they had agreed to this. So next day, we set off for a place of whose whereabouts I have not the slightest notion. We each carried a small bag of belongings. On arrival, our belongings were checked and taken from us. We were then ushered into a corridor and shown into what was nothing more than a prison cell. Before we could turn round, the door clanged to behind us.

It must be terrible to lose your liberty for committing a crime, but how much worse if you've done absolutely nothing to deserve it! My mother and I looked round this cell. High up on one wall was a small barred window and along each of two walls were a bed covered with a rough blanket and a solitary chair. In the corner near the door was a WC. There was nothing else except a spy-hole in the door through which eyes peered at us from time to time in sinister fashion.

I can only imagine my mother's feelings when she realised the situation we were in. I have to imagine them because she kept them strictly under control, no doubt to keep up my morale. We were shut off from the outside world with no information about why we were there, how long we would be kept there and what was to be our ultimate fate. Our only contact with another human being was when the door was briefly unlocked and we were handed our food by a grim-faced wardress. The only concession was a glass of milk for me because of my age.

So there we were in this small space with nothing to do and very little to do it with. We were totally thrown back on our own resources. I sometimes wonder how hostages and kidnap-victims fill their days, what ploys they use to stop themselves from going mad or hurling themselves fruitlessly against the walls of their cell. That was our problem too.

We coped by devising activities – anything to keep busy. We recited poems to each other, took turns at telling stories and played guessing-games. One of the few possessions we had been allowed to take into our cell was an illustrated calendar with a cartoon on each page. We made the situations in the cartoons into little dramas by expanding them and acting out the parts of the characters. One of the little plots involved a man with haemorrhoids.

'What are haemorrhoids, Mummy?' I asked.

My mother had to explain what they were and we chuckled over the little mimes we invented to keep up our spirits.

To make another game we cut a small cardboard box into oblong pieces with our dinner-knife. We then drew pictures on the pieces – two of each kind: two apples, two pears, two oranges, etc. With these we played a form of Snap. One of the pairs was labelled 'Mutti und Papa' – Mummy and Daddy – and when these appeared together I regarded it as an omen that we too would soon be together again and for a moment I clapped my hands with joy. On second thoughts, though, it was hard to keep back the tears and stifle the fear that, unlike in the fairy tales, such a happy ending did not seem very likely.

However much we tried to keep ourselves amused, time hung heavily upon us. We had been there for about four days when we were joined by a rather wild-looking woman in her thirties. I'm not sure whether she was there for a criminal offence – at any rate, she wasn't Jewish. Her presence meant that I had to sleep in the same narrow bed as my mother. She also brought an unpleasant odour into the cell. We ourselves were given a bowl of water to wash with each day and so were able to keep clean. The woman talked to my mother. I could not understand much of what she said, but it appeared that she had her period and needed to change her sanitary towel.

All this was news to me. I knew nothing about periods. In response to my insistent questioning about the expansion of my aunt's middle before the birth of her baby, my mother had told me 'Babies grow in their mummies' tummy'. She had stopped short of telling me how they got there and about menstruation. Now some explanation at least of periods was necessary. I doubt if I took much of it in, as my thoughts were elsewhere. I was wondering how long we would have to endure our loss of liberty, which seemed a much more important matter by comparison.

About two days later, the door of our cell opened and we were told we were to be released. What had happened to the idea of deporting us to Hungary I shall never know. My mother and I hugged each other in sheer relief and said goodbye to our cellmate. At the office we were given back our property. My mother, excited and overwrought as she must have been despite keeping up an outward appearance of calm, dropped something from her bag as we were leaving. It was a pretty glass powder-bowl her employer had given her. It lay in fifty brightly coloured fragments on the stone floor. She had treasured this bauble and now it was destroyed, along with so much else in our lives.

All things are relative. The reality that greeted us on our release was sombre enough, but at least we could see the sky, walk in the street and talk to a few people. Liberty is something you do not fully appreciate till you have lost it. Now that my father was gone, we did not return to our flat in the fifth district, but went to stay with my aunt Dora who made room for us in her small flat in the twentieth district. My mother and her sister were very close, so they must have derived some comfort from being together in such troubled times. I too enjoyed romping with my cousin Martin and playing with baby Norbert. They helped me to forget my worries for a while.

It was now June and a letter arrived, giving the date of my departure for England: we were to assemble at a Viennese railway station late on the night of 20 June. We were to bring a small suitcase packed with our belongings and there were to be no emotional farewells. Jews, it seemed, were not even to be allowed the luxury of expressing their grief at parting from their loved ones.

Preparations for the journey now began in earnest. My

Bundesunmittelbare Stadt **Wien.** Zahl: *l*

Schulbezirk: **Wien.** Schuljahr: 19 *37 / 38*

Schulnachricht

für *Imerdauer Martha,*

geboren am *2. Jänner* 19 *30* zu *Wien* in *—* , *mos.* Religion,

Schüler *in* der *2. b* Klasse der öffentlichen allgemeinen (vierklassigen) **Volksschule** für Knaben—Mädchen in Wien, *5.* Bezirk, *Margareten* - gasse straße Nr. *152* platz

Halbjahr	Betragen	Fleiß	Religion	Heimatkunde	Deutsche Sprache	Lesen	Schreiben	Rechnen und Raumlehre	Zeichnen (und Handarbeit)	Singen	Turnen (Körperliche Übungen)	Weibliche Handarbeiten	Äußere Form der Arbeiten	Zahl der versäumten Schultage		Zu spät gekommen	Tag der Ausstellung	Unterschrift der Eltern oder deren Stellvertreter
														entschuldigt	nicht entsch.			
I.	1	1	1	1	1	1	1	1	1	1	1	—	—	17	—	—	11. II. 1937	*Unterschrift*
II.																		

Auf Grund dessen wird diese *Schüler* [zum Aufsteigen in die nächsthöhere Klasse für

reif erklärt.

Hans Hochreß *Wilhelm Hanner,*
Leiter der Schule Klassenlehrer *in*

Wurde am 19 wegen Übersiedlung nach

abgemeldet. besucht die Volksschule seit 19 , ist hier eingetreten

am 19 und in heimatberechtigt.

Wien, am *Schulsiegel* Leiter der Schule.

Anmerkung: Die Befreiung vom Besuche eines oder mehrerer Unterrichtsgegenstände wird durch ein in die betreffende Spalte einzusetzendes „b" (befreit) ersichtlich gemacht.

Notenstufen.

a) Betragen:
1 = sehr gut
2 = gut
3 = entsprechend
4 = nicht entsprechend.

b) Fleiß, Fortgang und äußere Form der Arbeiten:
1 = sehr gut
2 = gut
3 = genügend
4 = nicht genügend.

Städt. Schuldruckforte. Form. III/1. — 50. 45. 12. 37.

An early school report shows Martha already scoring top grades

7277

This document of identity is issued with the approval of His Majesty's Government in the United Kingdom to young persons to be admitted to the United Kingdom for educational purposes under the care of the Inter-Aid Committee for children.

THIS DOCUMENT REQUIRES NO VISA.

PERSONAL PARTICULARS.

Name _IMMERDAUER, MARTHA_

Sex _FEMALE_ Date of Birth _2.7.30_

Place _WIEN_

Full Names and Address of Parents

IMMERDAUER ELIAS, PAULA

Brig. Leude 24

WIEN

The identity document issued to nine-year-old Martha enabling her to enter Britain in June 1939

mother found a small attaché case which in due course was packed with a few belongings: some underwear, a skirt and blouse, a dress and my most treasured possessions – the blonde doll that had been a present from my aunt in Belgium, some pictures of my parents, my autograph book and some of my favourite reading-books such as the *Arabian Nights* in German, printed in Gothic script. (I have it still.) My mother bought me an air-cushion to put under my head to sleep on, as the journey was likely to be a long one. Each stage of these preparations seemed like another little death, but by then I was too numb and shocked to put up any serious resistance.

My father was apparently still in the same police-prison in Vienna, and the day before I was due to leave, my mother took me to see him. We waited in a small office and eventually my father was brought in, flanked by two guards. He looked sad and unshaven, very different from the debonair man I had known as a little child. I don't remember much of what he said to me. What could he say? And what could I do? Scream, curse at this outrage? Throw my arms around him and refuse to leave? I did none of those things. He embraced me tenderly and wished me a safe journey. Then I saw my mother press some money into his hand as she kissed him goodbye before he was led away. That was my last sight of my father.

I lived through the next day as though in a trance – nothing seemed real any more. My case was packed, I said goodbye to my aunt and cousins and promised to write to them. My mother made me some ham sandwiches – a strange choice considering the Jewish taboo against pig-meat. I expect by then she had given up on the Jewish God and no longer thought it worth appeasing him. Or perhaps she had simply decided this was a practical way to stave off hunger on the journey.

That evening, my mother took me to the station. When we arrived, there were already large numbers of children and their parents there. I was surprised to see, despite our strict orders not to be emotional, a mother and daughter with their arms round each other's necks, both crying bitterly. But my mother and I kept to the rules: not a tear was shed. Suddenly, before the expected time, the great doors at the end of the waiting-room were swung back to reveal a platform with a train ready to be boarded. I embraced my mother for the last time. Then with a light suitcase, a heavy heart and a silly red hat that kept flopping into my face, I climbed into a compartment. It had several children of varying ages in it. Wearily I found a seat. Suddenly there was an outcry and a rush to the windows. Parents had been told that they must on no account follow their children on to the platform, but some, disobeying orders, had surged out of the waiting-room and on to the platform. Their children, spotting them joyfully, were able to wave a last goodbye. I scanned the sea of faces anxiously, hoping to have a last glimpse of my mother, but she wasn't there.

I must have been so weary (it was already late in the evening) and sick at heart that I took little notice of the other children in my compartment. I have no memory of how many there were or of their ages. All I know is that there were no adults in that part of the train to comfort or console, if indeed comfort or consolation were possible in those fraught circumstances. To all this was added the fact that I was a poor traveller at the best of times, apt to be sick on any moving vehicle, hence the long walks through the city of Vienna with my father who had learned to avoid any transport on wheels when in my company. Now it was all I could do to stop myself from heaving my supper – eaten some hours back – into my mouth. So I blew up the air-cushion, that last relic of my mother's loving care, and, leaning my head against the upholstery of the compartment, I must have dozed off for some time.

My next memory is of fleeting glimpses of a pleasant countryside and a broad river with green banks which the older children, now awake and vociferous, identified as the Rhine. At one point there was a rush to the windows to see the Lorelei rock. We had all learned the song of the Lorelei – the siren who, as the legend has it, lured infatuated sailors to their death on the rocks. So this was the place where her mischief was done! For a while this took our minds off the even greater mischief that was being done to us. Some of the older children now began to talk about their destination:

'I'm going to a town called Manchester!' or

'I'm going a long way north near Scotland!

'Where are you going?'

'Bow', I replied. 'It's a very nice part of London.'

Well, that is what I had been told and who was I to disbelieve it?

* * *

I remember very little else of that journey except that it took a long time and I had no idea of the direction I was travelling in. Other former refugees have described the relief of leaving Germany with the ever-present threat of hostile action by the SS and crossing the border into friendly Holland where there was apparently a welcome by Dutch people.

'We were welcomed back to humanity by humanity', one of these has written. But all of this passed me by. I was either too young or too sick to appreciate it.

What I do remember next is being put on board a big ship, bigger than the riverboat in which I had once sailed up the Danube to visit relatives in Budapest. Soon it was night again. By now I had completely lost count of the days. I found myself in a cabin with bunks and portholes and, presently, a swaying motion underneath me far worse than the rhythmic jogging of the train. Nevertheless, I must have slept fitfully despite the strange surroundings and when I woke up it was morning again. I imagine in response to some order we made our way up an unsteady staircase to a dining room where rows of tables covered in white cloths were prepared for us and we were given breakfast. I now made my acquaintance with small English sugar cubes. In Vienna sugar comes in larger lumps, and mistakenly thinking that I must double or treble the number of pieces I usually took to make up for the difference in size, I made my drink so sweet that it added to my already strong feeling of nausea. My ham sandwiches, hardly touched, were meanwhile decaying in the foodbag I had left in the cabin.

A little later came another shift, this time from the boat to a train which was waiting at the quayside. I realised vaguely that I was now in England, but had little idea of the route we had taken. Not till many years later did I discover that we had travelled northwards from Vienna, then along the Rhine and across Holland to the Hook and from there across the North Sea to Harwich. Now our luggage had to be put on the train by men with strange voices who were dressed in dark uniforms with peaked caps bearing the letters LNER. Here was a foreign land indeed! I tried out my English on one of these men. When I had asked my teacher what the word for a case was, she had said it was a 'trunk'. Coming from the wealthy family she did, that was no doubt a correct description of her luggage. But when I, clutching the pathetically small case that contained my belongings, said to the porter in my guttural accent, 'Where can I put my trunk?' he looked at me as though I was soft in the head.

Yet another journey, this time a shorter one. Then we arrived at a lofty station. I was by now completely bewildered and disorientated. I have vague impressions of being shepherded into a vast room where we were to wait to be collected by those responsible for our future welfare. I must have sat there for some time, my red hat slipping over my face and my head drooping with exhaustion until eventually I heard my name being called:

'Martha Immerdauer!'

I stumbled forward into the arms of a small, stout, middle-aged woman who said 'Martha?' I nodded as if to say 'Yes, that's me.'

As she took charge of my small amount of luggage (my sandwiches had long since been thrown away), I noticed that she had a companion, a taller, younger woman. They both propelled me towards an exit to start the journey to my foster mother's house. My most vivid recollections of that journey are twofold. I remember a wail of distress from the tall lady: she had laddered her best silk stockings and they would be expensive to replace. She felt this disaster keenly and made sure we knew about it. My other impression is of the occupational hazard of travelling with me: I was habitually sick on all forms of transport. I was sick on the bus we boarded, sick on the tube to which we switched till finally, in despair of getting me to her home that day, my foster mother took a taxi for the rest of the journey. Her companion had melted away at some point to mourn her stockings and return to her family.

5 • East End people and places

Having seen pictures of my foster mother dressed in a fur coat, I expected to be taken to, if not a stately, then at least an imposing home. However, my first view of my new home – as far as the condition of my stomach allowed me to register anything – was of a low, soot-blackened house in the middle of a row of similar dwellings with iron railings, funny bulging windows and steps down to a sunken part. I expected to be met by a maid, but the hall echoed eerily to our solitary footsteps.

My foster mother took me inside and, speaking to me in Yiddish, a language I could understand as it is a form of German, asked me what I wanted. *'Schlafen'* (sleep) was my succinct reply.

She then led me up a flight of stairs to a sparsely furnished room where there was a bed made up, and pointed to a chamberpot which I was to use, there being no upstairs lavatory. Morbidly shy about bodily functions, I balked at this crude intimacy. However, I must soon have fallen into an exhausted sleep.

Next morning, as the summer sun (it was now 23 June, three days after I had left Vienna) lit up my bedroom I awoke. When I saw the unfamiliar furniture – a wardrobe with inlaid pattern and mirror to match, a sewing-machine in a corner and a bed quite different from the narrow, white-painted bed I was used to sleeping in – the full realisation of what had happened to me hit me with overwhelming force. I was by myself at the age of nine in a strange house in a strange country with a strange language and worst of all, utterly separated from the parents I loved deeply and might never see again. I burst into floods of tears and was discovered in this state by my foster mother who did her best to comfort me.

She took me down to her kitchen, a small but pleasant room with pretty powder-blue curtains and a big table at which I sat down to a breakfast of banana and cream and English tea with milk. Both were unfamiliar though not unpalatable and I was careful this time not to overdo the sugar cubes. It was agreed that I would call my foster mother 'auntie'; not 'mother', she insisted, as I had a mother elsewhere. What that mother's feelings were as she made her way back from the station after seeing me off I can merely conjecture. I only hope that her sister, with whom she was staying, was able to give her some support.

Auntie then showed me round her house. It was what I was later to know as a Victorian terraced villa which she and her husband rented, the basement being sublet to a tenant. There were two bedrooms on the upper floor. The main one was furnished with a solid-looking bedroom suite in walnut. There was a large wardrobe, a gentleman's robe or tallboy, a cheval mirror, a dressing-table whose surface was covered with cut-glass trinkets and a wide double bed such as I had not seen before. There were mauve curtains, mauve rugs and a mauve bedspread. The second bedroom, less splendid and containing furniture of an older vintage, I have already described. There was no bathroom.

Downstairs at the front of the house were two reception rooms as they were grandly named. They were smallish rooms separated by folding doors furnished with disproportionately large mahogany furniture: an oval dining-table with heavy chairs to match supported by cabriole legs and a massive Queen Anne sideboard complete with mirror on its upper part. Lower down were deep cupboards and drawers and on their top surfaces sat two huge vases and two dancer-figurines with outspread skirts. A three-piece suite in hide, a Japanese gramophone cabinet, polished metal fenders and fire-irons and velvet curtains separated by a white net store-curtain with bobblefringe completed the decor. The floors of the rooms were covered by a carpet surrounded by polished linoleum.

I was soon to discover that these splendid rooms were in use only for special occasions. The kitchen was the place where we lived, ate and talked most of the time, sitting on hard upright chairs round the table which was the centre of the household. Latterly the sanctum sanctorum of the parlour had been disturbed by the arrival of a young man, a refugee from Berlin whom my foster parents had agreed to take in while they were waiting for me to come. He had outstayed this time and was now being put up on the settee in the front room. This my aunt regarded as a great concession.

The rest of the house consisted of three basement rooms. To get downstairs from our part of the house you had to negotiate a dark and steep staircase situated near the kitchen. At the bottom of the stairs was a hall which was in permanent darkness and beyond this, a door led to the lavatory, a little hut in the yard. Before you went down, you took with you some pieces of toilet paper from a roll that was kept upstairs and wasteful excess of this commodity was discouraged. In this shadowy territory lived a young family: a very young woman who used to curl her straight hair with hot tongs, her husband who was in the Territorial Army and rode a motor-cycle and their pale-looking son. Perhaps this basement flat was their stepping-stone to better things, but I used to shudder as I approached their subterranean quarters.

That evening I met my foster father for the first time. I had missed seeing him the previous evening, as I had been asleep when he got in from work. He was a small, slim, mild-mannered man with a twinkle in his eye. His pale blue eyes, sparse sandy hair and straight features made him look much less Jewish than his wife. I found out that they were both born in Poland – she in Plotsk, a small town near Warsaw and he in a village near the East Prussian border, which meant that he could speak some German. Both had emigrated to England before the First World War. Like many of their contemporaries, they had left Poland for good reason – the endemic anti-Semitism that oppressed the Jewish population and goaded the braver ones to seek a better life abroad.

Having lost his parents at an early age, my foster father had come to England on his own and met and married his wife in London. He had worked as a tailor in an East End sweatshop for many years before deciding to change his trade. Using a bicycle he had worked hard to acquire the rigorous knowledge of the streets of London demanded of taxi-drivers and had eventually passed out as a licensed cabbie. The solid respectability of my foster parents' home had been built on the improved wages and greater independence he had thus won for himself.

I remember him as a simple but loving man. He spoke several languages – English, Polish, Yiddish and some German, yet he had few words. Despite his limited horizons (neither he nor his wife had had any formal education in Poland), he was utterly reliable and managed to radiate good humour and enjoyment in any company. He had a few characteristic jokes: if someone asked him,

'Would you like another cup of tea?'
he would reply,
'No, I'd like more tea in the same cup.'

With such mundane ploys he lightened the atmosphere and kept us cheerful.

The only times I can remember him being really angry was when news reached us of some fresh Nazi atrocity. 'Bastards!' he would exclaim, digging his fork savagely into his supper. To me he was unfailingly patient and kind. How much he understood of the complexities of my situation I have no idea, but his broad humanity was a shield against a savage world.

His name was Woolf, but my aunt called him 'Willie', and this was sometimes shortened by English people to 'Will'. His surname was 'Greensztein', a mixture of German and English elements with an intrusive Polish 'z'. This mirrored the complex identity of a man brought up, like many other Jews, astride a number of different cultures and language traditions.

51

Later he shortened his name to 'Green', but in official communications it remained 'Greenstein'.

During the week he would come home from work wearing an old cloth cap and with his cabbie's badge dangling from the lapel of the coat he wore most of the year to keep out the draught from the open side of his vehicle. I had no notion of the stress and hardship of his working-life in London's traffic. If he complained of being tired, I would say in childish ignorance: 'But you're only sitting down all the time in a cab!' And he would reprove me gently if at all.

On Friday there was a transformation: it was his custom to leave work early, have a bath at the local public baths and change out of his workaday clothes into a dark suit. My aunt spread a laundered damask cloth on the table for the traditional Sabbath meal of chicken noodle soup, braised chicken with potatoes, green vegetables and a compote of fruit. Before the meal she lit two white candles set in tall brass candlesticks and said a blessing over them as my mother had done. Then, incongruously, my uncle would drink a glass of his favourite beer and I some lemonade. There was something immensely reassuring about these rituals.

Although my aunt's house was not as grand as I had imagined it would be, I was fascinated by some of her mod-cons. There was an electric iron (my mother had a gas one), an electric heater sparingly used in winter and a vacuum cleaner. (My mother used to beat her rugs on a line in the courtyard of our flats with a cane beater, emitting clouds of dust.) My aunt, though uneducated, was socially gregarious, so that there were often callers to her home. In addition to this, any outdoor activity such as whitening the front steps with a special powder gave the excuse for morning chats with neighbours in overalls and carpet slippers and with curlers peeping from their turbaned heads. For me, one of the most intriguing sights was the milkman delivering bottled milk from a crate in his cart; while he put the milk on one doorstep, his horse would trot unbidden to the next. What with the gossiping women, the milkman's cry, the bell of the rag and bone man and the call of the knife-grinder, this little turning off the Bow Road was abuzz with community life.

I had brought few clothes with me, so my aunt took me to the local market and bought me two summer dresses and a blazer with silver buttons and a tartan hair ribbon. I was very proud of these and remember describing them to my mother in a letter. In answer to her anxious enquiries about my health and well-being, I painted a rosy picture. Perhaps these letters brightened her sad lot a little. They gave me little opportunity to express my homesickness and sorrow, but cheerfulness was the order of the day, so who was I to go against it?

Two days after my arrival, my aunt decided I needed to be with children of my own age. Never one to let the grass grow under her feet, she marched me up to the houses of two neighbours and, in obedience to her command, two girls trooped out to play with me in the street. We played bouncing games against the air raid shelter that was already in place at the top of the street; then more ball-games on the pavement (there was no traffic in sidestreets apart from the occasional horse and cart, so playing was safe). Then one of the girls produced a skipping-rope and we had a few turns at this. There was little I could say to them, so we smiled and nodded at each other.

Finally one of them asked: 'Are you tired?'

I had no idea what this meant, so I must have looked blank. Now there followed a series of mimes: they let their heads droop and closed their eyes and put their hands to the side of their heads. Thinking that this was like the game of 'statues' I had played in Vienna, I imitated everything they did and was surprised by their look of exasperation. In the end one of the girls took me to her mother who said to me in Yiddish: 'Di bist mid?'

Light dawned and I replied: 'Ja, ich bin müde', much to everybody's relief.

Later that week, I began to get to know my new surroundings. I made the acquaintance of the grocershop in the Bow Road where my aunt bought most of her provisions. The shopkeeper was a bespectacled, middle-aged woman with wavy grey hair swept back into a bun. Her hairstyle was as severe as the grey overall she always wore. I was fascinated by the contrast between her and her daughter who occasionally disported herself in the shop. It was like seeing a black crow next to a peacock. I was greatly impressed by the daughter's elegant clothes, fashionable hairstyle and a peculiar yellow face powder she always wore.

My aunt often sent me to this shop on errands for special items. 'A quarter of smoked salmon from the belly', I would be told to ask for, and the grocer-lady would smile in understanding. My aunt was not to be fobbed off with inferior cuts.

Across the road lived two other little girls, Frances and Joan, with whom I played at the weekend. Their mother and my aunt seemed particularly friendly. One day my aunt told me that I was to be looked after by another neighbour as she and the mother of the little girls were going to the 'London Chest'.

'Whose chest?' I enquired.

'The London Chest Hospital in Victoria Park,' was the reply. I was more mystified than ever. To my surprise, on the appointed afternoon both ladies went off together, dressed in their best summer edge-to-edge coats, smart court shoes and silk stockings. My aunt returned with a look of satisfaction and a huge bottle of amber liquid. The visit obviously combined the function of social outing and proof of the world's solicitude: a medicine to make them better.

Medicines, in fact, played a great part in my aunt's life. Soon after my arrival, she had quizzed me:

'Did you have your bells open?' What bells she meant I could not imagine.

'Have you been to the WC?' she persisted.

Gradually I discovered that she meant my bowels and hastened to answer her in the affirmative. If ever I said no, a battery of remedies would be brought out. There was the chocolate laxative, Exlax, or Syrup of Figs, or for really obstinate bowels, Brooklax, which was supposed to have some of the properties of dynamite. I found out what the strange smell in her bedroom was: it came from the liniments she used to anoint her rheumatic limbs. In the cupboard by her bed was a veritable arsenal of nostrums – Zambuk and Germolene, iodine for cuts, Andrews' Liver Salts for indigestion and a whole lot more. For me this was a new experience. A black ointment the doctor had prescribed for my father for some foot-trouble and a bottle of aspirins were all the drugs I could remember in my parents' home.

Bow, where my foster parents lived, was technically part of the East End of London, but a little removed from districts like Whitechapel and Stepney where the Jewish immigrants had originally settled. There they had found cheap lodgings in cramped and often bug-infested quarters when they 'came off the onion-boat' as they humorously put it, having made the journey from Russia or Poland or Lithuania. Names of East End streets cropped up frequently in their conversation, so I got to know Black Lion Yard (pronounced blecklenyud) Hessel Street, the Lane (Petticoat Lane). These were relics of a history I did not share but which seemed important to the grown-ups.

One day soon after my arrival in England my aunt took me to see her friend Raisl (Rosie) in the real East End. The bus route was along a noisy and busy main road flanked by small shop-fronts, warehouses and workshops displaying their names on signboards attached to their crumbling facades. We then walked down a side turning containing a row of very low-slung terraced Victorian labourers' cottages whose front doors opened directly onto the street. Once inside, we stepped into a narrow passage-way. I noticed that the floor was covered with worn linoleum and the walls encased in smoke-blackened wallpaper. Beyond the first door on the left we were shown into the parlour which contained the 'best' furniture and a display of family photographs. There were images in sepia of bridegrooms in evening-suits and brides in long white dresses against an elegant balustrade – courtesy of Boris the photographer. Soon, however, we were invited into the real centre of the household, the kitchen. Our hostess was a widow, thick of girth and short of breath. She wore a capacious overall which protected most of her stocky body. I was fascinated by her walk – a bandy-legged wobble from side to side as she made us tea in her crowded kitchen while her sons argued about politics in another corner. She had obviously had a hard life, yet there was warmth in her still piercing violet eyes and welcome in her manner.

Another time I was asked to give a message to my aunt's friend Golda who lived round the corner. This meant walking alongside the cemetery at the bottom of our street. I tried to keep to the sunny side, avoiding too close a look at the blackened tombstones that protruded from the railings as well as the cracks in the pavement. My aunt's friend lived with her old mother, a silent, inscrutable figure swathed in layers of clothing despite the summer season. On her head she had the smooth brown, artificial-looking hair I recognised as belonging to the kind of wig worn by orthodox Jewish women. She sat there still and expressionless, while her daughter chatted volubly to me.

I lived in these surroundings for only a short time and became aware of the gradations of poverty they represented. My abiding impression, however, is of a feeling of community, of friendliness, neighbourliness. It would have been difficult to feel utterly alone and abandoned in such a setting.

I have not so far described my foster mother, 'auntie', in detail. Her name was Annie, adapted from the Hebrew Hannah. She was in her forties, a diminutive figure scarcely five feet tall. She had softly waving hair whose even brown colour owed something to henna framing a round face, eyes twinkling benignly behind tortoiseshell spectacles, a broad nose with flaring nostrils and thin lips. An ample bosom, thick waist and hips on slim legs made her look like a puffball on two slender stalks. She made up for this unprepossessing shape by a very upright carriage and purposeful movements. Orphaned at an early age in Poland, she had had the courage to make the journey alone in her teens to a foreign country in search of a better future. Her horizons were narrow – she could neither read nor write – and her knowledge was limited to practical affairs, yet she had a fund of shrewdness which enabled her to survive many vicissitudes.

She was quite fluent in everyday English, but still retained a slight foreign accent. 'W' was a difficult sound for her and occasionally she mispronounced words, as she had no means of checking their accuracy. At home she spoke in a mixture of English, Yiddish and Polish, the last particularly when she did not want me to understand. However, I could usually guess from the expressions and gestures that accompanied her words the gist of the subject she intended to conceal. My uncle had a calming effect on his volatile wife, toning down her excesses with quiet words. One Polish expression I heard him utter several times intrigued me so that I asked what it meant. It sounded like 'Daye spokoi byidna jezko' and I was told it meant 'leave the poor child alone', no doubt his method of cutting short some complaint about my behaviour.

My foster mother had desperately wanted to have children of her own, but had been unlucky enough to lose several babies in stillbirths and miscarriages. Fortunately for us both, her strong need to express her maternal feelings dovetailed with my need for comfort and security at a very stressful time in my life.

Unlike my natural mother, my foster mother had her emotions close to the surface. She would burst into cries of 'oi veh!' when a neighbour confided some trouble. I have memories of her on the phone commiserating with a cousin whose daughter was about to have an operation with a series of appalled clickings of the tongue. Not to be outdone, she contributed some minor mishap of her own to the stock of woes with the oft-repeated phrase 'Sarah, you doino' (don't know), which became a catch-phrase for me. She babbled freely about her illnesses – double lamonia (pneumonia), essmen-bronchitis (asthma and bronchitis) and rheumatism. She was warm-hearted and easily moved, but could curse viciously in Yiddish anyone she suspected of slighting her.

One aspect of her openness I found disturbing: soon after my arrival I heard her saying to a neighbour: 'She cried bitterly. It broke my heart.' I already knew enough English by then to understand what she had said. To have my most private emotions made public outraged my stubborn pride. After this incident I put a firm lid on my feelings to prevent a repetition of this betrayal.

Meanwhile my struggles with an unfamiliar world continued. Posters, road signs, street names – all were strange to me. I let my eyes linger with relief on the few names that I could regard as old friends: Odol toothpaste, Nivea Creme, Maggi soup cubes, but there was little else from my earlier incarnation I could recognise. Even the windows were different: they moved up and down on things called sash-cords which were always giving trouble, instead of simply opening outwards like the ones in my parents' flat. I was still thinking in German and communicating in German with my foster parents. However, apart from the boy from Berlin and a friend of my foster parents who recited a few cynical verses he had picked up during a stay in Germany, I had no contact with anyone from home. Occasionally the radio would resound to the strains of the 'Blue Danube' or 'Wien, Wien nur du allein' sung with a throbbing vibrato by Richard Tauber. These touched hidden springs of emotion, but I could not abandon myself to this Viennese Schwärmerei, for how can you allow yourself to feel nostalgic about a country that has so utterly rejected you?

My days were quite crowded with new experiences, so I hardly had time to miss the books I would have been reading if I had still been in Vienna. What irked me, though, was being cut off from the mainstream of events. Newspapers were no longer accessible to me and I found the radio at first a confusing babble. In ordinary conversation people talked too fast for me to be able to work out more than the gist of what they were saying. I, on the other hand, had to choose my words slowly and carefully to make myself understood in English. I had asked my English teacher in Vienna what words to say if I couldn't follow what people were saying, and the phrase she taught me, 'I don't understand', was very useful in the early days.

1 The author's grandmother as a young woman

2 The author's father with his mother and sister in Budapest during the
First World War. He is wearing the uniform of an Austrian Army officer

3 The author's parents, Elias and Paula Immerdauer, Vienna, 1939

4 Cousins Martin (aged four) and Norbert, born in 1939, photographed in Vienna shortly before the outbreak of war. These photographs were sent to their cousin Martha, by then evacuated to England in the *Kindertransport*

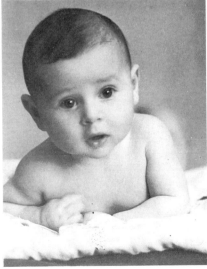

5 The last holiday before the war began: Martha with her foster parents Will and Annie Greensztein, on the beach at Cliftonville, August 1939

6 With foster mother (and an inanimate dog) on the sea-front at Margate

7 Growing up in England:
aged 14 (left) in 1944
8 . . . and aged 18 (right) in
1948, the year Martha left
school for university. That
summer she was invited
on holiday in Cornwall by
relatives of her mother, who
had settled in Redruth after
the war

9 The Cornwall relations:
Eva and her daughter Helen

10 The Sixth Form at Dalston County School, 1948. Martha is second from the right in the front row

11 The author with her husband and sons, Jonathan and Tony, 1958

12 One relative who survived the Holocaust was Martha's Aunt Irene, who with her husband Sigmund emigrated to Palestine before the war. Their son served as a sergeant in the British Army and their daughter had a baby in 1948. In 1970 Martha was able to visit Aunt Irene in Israel and learned more about her lost family on her father's side.

Going to the cinema could have its frustrations too. It seemed that in London every high street rejoiced in picture palaces grandly named Plaza or Paramount or Regent. Their softly carpeted interiors were not so much a home-from-home as a brief trip into a luxurious dream-world. I remember being taken to see a long programme which included *The Wizard of Oz*. I enjoyed the pictures and Judy Garland's singing, but kept losing the thread of the story. When my aunt yielded to my demand for explanations, there would be a loud 'Shhhh!' from the row behind.

Some of the food I was given was also strange. Not all – chicken noodle soup and bortsch (beetroot soup) I had eaten at home – but sea-fish was a new flavour. In a land-locked country like Austria the only available fish were bland-tasting river-fish like carp or pike. It took me some time to get used to the strong taste of the weird flat shape called plaice, especially when served cold in a batter with the ubiquitous Heinz tomato ketchup. I missed my mother's *Wiener Schnitzel* and mince wrapped in cabbage-leaves. On the whole, though, as I got more accustomed to it, I found that my aunt's repertoire of dishes, though limited, was reasonably tasty and well-cooked.

Thursday was the day my aunt did her shopping for the Sabbath and I accompanied her on her expeditions to the local market. Once arrived, she would scrutinise the birds on the poultry-stall to find one that was of the condition and size she wanted. Then would follow some haggling, with my aunt expressing outrage at the price demanded, and the stallholder predicting ruin for her family if she lowered it any further. All this was done in a sharp Yiddish vernacular with appropriate gestures. When this shadow-boxing was over and a price agreed, the bird would be plucked and wrapped in newspaper.

Back at home, the first task was to slit the bird open and remove the intestines and any other unwanted parts. Sometimes there were little round yellow eggs inside which could be cooked in the soup. Then the bird would be salted and left to drain on a wooden board to make it kosher. When this process was finished, the cooking could begin, and here

59

the trick was not to waste a single morsel. First the bird was cut into quarters. Then the legs (*pulkas*) and the wings (*fliegel*) were separated. The skin would be singed to remove any small hairs or quills left by the market-woman. Then the giblets would be put into a pot with water and a few vegetables to make the soup. Next, the skin of the neck had to be stuffed with a mixture of flour, fat and seasoning and added to the soup-pot. Finally, the fat had to be clarified. This, when heated, would melt down to an amber liquid, and, when cooled, to a yellow paste which could be used in cooking. A residue of little crisp brown nuggets of fat would be left unclarified (*greeven*) and these were delicious when salted and spread on rye bread.

* * *

I was beginning to find my way about my new surroundings, but socially I still felt like an oddity. My very name attracted comment. Some people, seeing me, would burst out singing 'Martha, rambling rose of the wild wood!' I found this both flattering and embarrassing. Then they would express puzzlement at my having such an old-fashioned name, as it seemed to them, a name associated in their minds with Victorian spinsters and servants. Why my parents had chosen it I had then no idea, but I found out later from my aunt in Israel that I had been named after a favourite sister of my father's who had been called Marya.

At this time, whether my aunt had had enough of my undiluted company or whether she felt that being with children of my own age would be good for me, she decided to send me to school, despite the fact that the end of term was near. I found myself, therefore, in a class of primary school pupils doing work which was incomprehensible to me. There was arithmetic for a start, a subject which at home had held no terrors for me, but which added to my problems now. Brought up on the metric system, I tended to do my sums in tens, but found to my dismay that this didn't work with English money. Farthings, halfpennies, pence, shillings and pounds – each had to be treated differently. As for measurements, on the

Continent they were in convenient tens and hundreds. This was no help at all when it came to rods, poles, perches, chains and furlongs, all of which had idiosyncratic lengths unconnected with any logic I could fathom. It seemed that calculating had to be learned afresh, as if learning a new language was not enough! I suppose I should have been grateful that at least the alphabet was more or less the same.

Coming home with a wealth of new impressions, words, songs, I demanded explanations from my aunt and uncle, unaware of the limitations of their own knowledge.

'What's father temsis?' I asked one day after a singing lesson.

'Father temsis? No such ting', replied my uncle.

'Yes, there is!' I insisted. 'We sang it today: old father temsis rolling along down to the mighty sea.' Bewilderment all round.

Another time Werner, the young man from Berlin who was still staying with us and was learning the tailoring trade, asked for a 'simble' – as he pronounced it in his German accent. My uncle smiled indulgently. 'Not "simble" – "timble"', he corrected.

The object in question was, of course, a thimble, the English 'th' sound eluding both of them. I soon realised that, kind and affectionate though my foster parents were, they were not reliable dictionaries. I put my trust instead in the BBC, which became my lifeline for accurate language-learning.

School was now winding down and instead of formal lessons there were singing and dancing sessions. These gave me my first contact with English and American popular songs. One girl volunteered to sing 'Pennies from Heaven' complete with American accent, raising her arms aloft to illustrate the theme. Another girl sidled to the front of the class to sing a song that began with the words 'Oh, Johnny, oh, Johnny How you can love!' Her singing was accompanied by knowing winks and rollings of the eyes as she swung her chubby hips in time to its rhythm. To a prudish nine-year-old like me this precocious sexuality was embarrassing. Other children sang

61

'Any Umberellas' and 'Underneath the Arches', songs popularised by Flanagan and Allen. All were a far cry from the Viennese lilts I was accustomed to.

The girls in the class were also practising some dances to be performed to their mothers on the last day of term. They twirled and clapped and made arches in time to dances with titles like 'Gathering Peasecods' and 'Dashing White Sergeant'. Nobody tried to teach me the steps which were already familiar to the other pupils. Noticing my look of dismay when it became clear that I would not be able to participate in this entertainment, my teacher gave me a tiny part in the proceedings: I was to put on a long dress and pretend to be the tutor of the dancers. So, on the appointed day, I stepped forward in full view of the assembled parents, my aunt among them, made a deep curtsey towards them and with a sweeping but unscheduled gesture, beckoned to the dancers to come forward while I took my own seat ceremoniously. After all, it was not in my nature to allow myself to be totally ignored.

Now school was over and thoughts turned to the holidays. My parents had had few such luxuries. An occasional day by the Danube or a trip up the river were all the treats I could remember. The idea of spending two whole weeks in a hotel – boarding-house actually – seemed very exciting. There were preparations and new purchases to be made: a white jacket for my aunt and white canvas shoes and a bathing-costume for me. We were going to the seaside! For me, after living nine years in Central Europe and encountering the sea only en route for England, this was something to look forward to. Cases were brought out, tickets purchased. One couldn't help being caught up in this atmosphere of anticipated enjoyment.

However, there were darker signs on the horizon as well. 'We'll do so and so if only there isn't a war' was an oft-repeated phrase. Nobody wanted war and the then Prime Minister, Mr Chamberlain, had promised his people 'peace in our time' after his visit to Hitler in Munich. Nobody then realised that 'peace in our time' would turn out to be 'peace for a year' only, but the aggressive build-up of German arms was evident to those who could really face the facts.

In the sky I noticed some podgy grey objects like giant inflated toys. 'What are those things up there?' I enquired.

'Barrage balloons', I was told. 'If God forbid there was a war and an enemy aeroplane tried to bomb us, it would get caught up in the cables under those things and crash to the ground.'

I was in no way able to assess the efficacy of this defence, but it brought home to me the ever-present possibility of war, and with it, the cutting-off of all communication with my mother. Another ominous sign was the air raid shelter already in place at the top of our street, a brick structure whose interior smelt of damp and stale air. Round the walls were slatted benches, but no other furniture. The outside was useful for bouncing-games. Once our curiosity about the interior was satisfied, we children were not tempted to linger there.

Then there were the beams of light criss-crossing the sky. I had seen similar ones in Vienna and when I asked what they were, my mother had tried to reassure me by pretending they were a form of advertisement for one of the big stores. Now, in England, I was told the truth: 'They're searchlights. Their job is to pick out enemy aeroplanes so that our guns can shoot them down.'

Parents had also been told of arrangements for evacuating children out of London in the event of war. All these preparations were enough to cast a shadow on any holiday plans, yet people were determined to enjoy what was left of that fateful summer while they could.

The English seaside! This was a totally new experience for me. Once again I was in a strange bedroom, but for a happier reason. All around us as we made our way to the dining-room were welcoming smiles. The staff of the hotel knew my uncle and aunt from previous years and the blonde waitress lingered at our table to exchange pleasantries and banter with my uncle who seemed to be popular there.

After lunch I had my first sight of the beach. The resort was not named Cliftonville for nothing, for to get to the sea you had to negotiate steep cliffs by means of a cable-lift that spanned the drop from promenade to beach. My uncle found some deck-chairs while my aunt took off my summer dress, revealing the bathing-costume I had been told to put on underneath it. She then anointed me with a sticky oil on my pale exposed neck, arms and legs. After that, we threaded our way barefoot between the sunbathers over the glassy dry sand and the softer damp sand to the edge of the waves which bubbled gently over our feet. Despite the warm weather, the water felt cold. Unable to swim, I had to content myself with paddling, dabbling my feet in little rock pools and admiring the elaborate constructions some children had made in the sand. Later that week, armed with a rubber ring I tried to follow my aunt's instructions for making some rudimentary swimming-movements, but was too scared to take my feet off the bottom. When we returned to the hotel my feet were itchy with sand and my back smarted with sunburn despite the oil, but a cool bath, plentiful dabbings with calamine lotion and a good supper had a soothing effect.

Next day I made the acquaintance of a structure that jutted out to sea – the pier. We walked along its wooden floor, inhaling the salty, seaweed-fresh air. In a booth at one side were some machines with flashing lights and others containing glass cases that held a variety of treasures resting on a pebbly floor. A miniature crane promised to deliver one of these to you when you put your coin in the slot, but alas! after some moments of tension when the prize seemed almost in your hand, it slipped out of the lax grip of the claws of the crane which dredged up only a few pebbles or at best, a consolation-prize of a sugar-coated sweet.

I had never had so many new experiences in such a short time. There were the cones of Lyons ice cream – not a patch on the Italian ice-creams I was used to in Vienna, but welcome none the less. There was candyfloss – a more attractive sight than taste – and rock with its intriguing lettering going right through the stick. Outside some of the shops that lined the seafront selling quoits and beach-shoes and buckets and spades were carousels of postcards with views of the bay and 'wish you were here' inscriptions. Garishly coloured comic postcards specialised in showing enormous women dominating weedy little men. One depicted a solicitor with hands outstretched under the ample bosom of a lady client. It bore the caption:

'Madam, do you wish to place your affairs in my hands?'

I nagged for an explanation of the word 'affairs', but didn't understand the joke till some years later.

Along the promenade boats were moored. In front of them were boards advertising trips along the coast. My aunt, only too well aware of my limitations as a traveller, knew better than to tempt Providence by taking me on one of these. Instead we made our way to the bandstand where there were late-afternoon concerts. We sang along with the band to popular tunes like 'Somewhere over the Rainbow'. I learned the cho-ruses and shouted 'Oi!' with the rest of the audience at the end of the 'Lambeth Walk'. Another time I tried my hand at getting the ball into the holes in the putting-green, had my photo-graph taken on a stuffed donkey and a ride on the sands on a real donkey. I could have done with some other children for company, but my aunt and uncle were determined to make this a happy holiday, so it would have been churlish not to show appreciation of their efforts by joining in the fun.

Always at the back of my mind was the question of how my mother was faring and what was happening to my father. I wrote a long letter home to try to cheer my mother up. I felt twinges of guilt at enjoying myself when I could imagine that in Vienna each day brought new anxieties for those left behind. Knowing the circumstances, I had no expectation of seeing my parents soon, but hoped against hope that they would be safe and that one day we would be reunited. My strongest feeling when I arrived in England, apart from the homesickness that threatened to overwhelm me, had been relief – relief that I could lay my head on my pillow at night without listening for that aggressive knock on the door. It caused me great grief that my parents were not able to share this sense of security.

6 • *Evacuation and air raids*

When the two weeks of our holiday were over, it was time to make tracks for London. The newspaper headlines brought us back to a reality far removed from beaches and candyfloss. Getting a gas mask and buying blackout material were now the immediate preoccupations of the grown-ups. Then came news that the scheduled evacuation of London schoolchildren would take place in two days' time. Once again my case was packed and with my gas mask slung over my shoulder and a label on my blazer, my aunt took me to join a crocodile of similarly equipped children in the playground of our school.

Standing there I had a strong sense of *déjà vu*: crowds of children, hand-luggage, farewells – hadn't I braced myself to endure this before? I decided then and there that enough was enough. So when my aunt tried to propel me towards the other children, I dug in my heels and said: 'I'm not going!'

'But you'll be with your friends. All the others are going. Anyway, it won't be for long.'

But not all the coaxing and cajoling could make me change my mind.

'I don't care about the others. I'm not a parcel. I'm not going with them.'

My aunt, with an insight that was not altogether typical of her, gave in, and we trotted home to her little house in Bow where my uncle greeted us with surprise. A few days later my aunt and uncle evacuated themselves with me and I was spared the trauma of a second separation.

* * *

Of the problems created by my refusal to be evacuated with the other children I had no notion. I had little idea of money. All I knew was that my parents did not have enough of it to get out of Austria and my foster parents seemed to have just enough of it to rub along fairly comfortably. I had not connected this fact with my uncle's work as a licensed London cabbie. Nor had I realised that this meant he would not easily find work elsewhere.

However, with war imminent and London an obvious target for bombing, all energies were now concentrated on getting out. The tenants in the basement had vanished – the young man to join his regiment and his wife and son to relatives in the country. Werner, the boy from Berlin, had at last managed to get an affidavit to emigrate to the United States and had set sail in the *Queen Mary*. So we packed our clothes and essential belongings, locked up the house and took a taxi – not my uncle's – to Paddington Station. We were heading for Paignton in Devon. The reason for this choice was the fact that my aunt's cousins were already there and my aunt no doubt felt that she needed to be surrounded by some familiar faces. We arrived at Paddington Station amid a scene of frantic activity: there were porters rushing about with piles of luggage on trolleys, huge queues at the ticket office and clusters of young men with duffle-bags off to join the forces. The platform was packed with people embracing and saying goodbye to relatives they were leaving behind in London as they too sought safety in the west country.

Our first lodgings were in a small boarding-house. After a long journey we arrived late and tired and met the cousins who were staying in another part of the same house. They had been preparing for bed and were in their dressing-gowns. Our supper was a hasty snack on a tray in yet another strange bedroom. To me everything was bewilderingly topsy-turvy, the only constant being the reassuring presence of my foster parents. After the first week it became obvious that as a permanent solution to our housing problems the guest-house was too expensive, so the grown-ups set about looking for an unfurnished house to rent that would accommodate several families. They found one at the top of a little hill in a turning off the main road and proceeded to furnish it with job-lots from a local auction room.

We were three families: cousin Max, a portly oldish man, and his wife, Miriam, a slim lady with the stately upswept hairstyle made popular by Queen Mary; their daughter Helen, and her baby of six months, Melanie. Finally there were my uncle and aunt and myself. When the house was ready for occupation, we all moved in. There was no attempt to make the house beautiful, and only basic necessities had been bought. The living-room had a collection of ancient and unmatching chairs, and the sofa under its faded chintz cover had a big dip in the middle. Pride of place was given to the wireless, which was in a large brown case with a rounded top and sported massive dials. We listened to this avidly for news of the war.

The grown-ups each had some sort of bedroom furniture, but my room was the smallest and bleakest of all. There was just space for an iron bedstead and a single chair. The walls were distempered a sickly pea-green and the floor was covered with green lino. There was nothing else. Compared with what people in Europe were going through this was little cause for complaint, but I can't help a frisson as I remember the dreariness and chill of that little room.

Every night before going to bed I would pray to God in German to keep my parents safe, adding the short Hebrew prayer asking for God's protection that my father had taught me. I used to make this supplication in bare feet on the cold lino in the hope that it would stand a better chance of reaching the ear of the Almighty. I kept this up for several weeks, but when there was no dramatic response, I weakened in my resolve and henceforth said my prayers in the comparative comfort of my bed.

We had already listened, saddened though not surprised, to Chamberlain's declaration of war. Poland had been ruthlessly invaded by the powerful German army and everything was now being geared to the prospect of a long conflict. Blackout curtains and shutters had to be fitted to all windows so that no light could penetrate outside to help enemy aircraft find their targets. Gas masks had to be carried everywhere. These were issued in cardboard boxes that soon disintegrated, so there was quite a trade in more permanent cases. These ranged from expensive pigskin ones with torches inside for the wealthy, to cheap imitation-leather ones for the rest of us. As for the mask itself, it had a rubber shape that fitted over the front of your hair and forehead, a perspex panel over your eyes to enable you to see out and a metal disc rather like a pig's snout that rested below your nose and mouth and was designed to filter the gas and let you breathe cleaner air. The whole apparatus had a nasty rubbery smell when you put it on and we all hoped that we would not have to use it in earnest. Another necessary piece of equipment was a torch to penetrate the darkness of the blackout. Number 8 batteries, which served the kind of torches most commonly used, were much in demand so that there would be a run on any shop rumoured to have supplies.

Gradually our families settled down together. There was only one bathroom, but there was no competition for this. With taps that produced only cold water and a room-temperature that was far from inviting, we usually preferred to wash in our bedrooms with the aid of hot kettles and a bowl. Nevertheless, Friday night was designated bath-night. We took it in turns to put shillings in a slot to activate the geyser. This rusty object rumbled and hissed and spat out first a brown trickle and then enough warm water to cover part of your body.

The women had to share the kitchen and we all congregated in the living-room. The problem here was that my aunt's cousin, being more orthodox than the rest of us, would not allow any Jewish member of the household to light the fire on the Sabbath. The solution was to pay the son of a non-Jewish neighbour to do the job for us. I could not see the logic of this, but was grateful for the warmth of the fire, which you could just feel if you were close enough to it.

For me the outbreak of the war had been particularly devastating. I could no longer write to my mother in what was now an enemy country. What had once meant safety was now in danger and I imagined the German hordes would soon sweep over us. To my surprise, however, the grown-ups took a calmer view of the situation. Nevertheless, the signs of war were now everywhere. The eldest sons of two other relatives of my aunt's who also lived nearby were called up and joined the Royal Air Force. (I found out later that one of them had the dangerous job of rear-gunner in a Spitfire.) The bathing-huts on the sea-front had been replaced by conical tank-traps made of concrete and the promenade bristled with barbed wire. On the green in front of one of the big hotels newly recruited RAF men wheeled and marched to a drum-beat. As they returned to their quarters they sang or whistled a jolly tune with the refrain

I've got tuppence to lend and tuppence to spend
And tuppence to send home to my wife.

Morale had to be kept up at all costs.

It was obvious then that my uncle could not stay with us any longer. We were living on savings and they were running out. So, in company with the other men in my aunt's extended family, he returned to work in London during the week. As two of my aunt's relatives were prosperous opticians and owned what was then a rare luxury, a private motorcar, Friday evening brought a carload of men eager to join their wives and families. It was the time of the 'phony war'; nothing much was happening in London or anywhere else for that matter, so that although this strategy was not without risk, it was the only possible compromise between the need for togetherness and the need to earn a living. When he returned from London my uncle always brought us a special treat; for me it was usually some of my favourite toffee with nuts inside.

My first playmates in Paignton were three boys, the younger sons of two other cousins of my aunt whose parents lived nearby. They did me the favour of including a mere girl in their games – usually football – in a muddy lane near our house when the weather was dry. My position was invariably in goal which I found only slightly less boring than being indoors with the grown-ups. On wet days, however, there were more interesting pursuits. We played Monopoly, a game I had not come across in Austria. My playmates, being older than me and the sons of real entrepreneurs, were adept at buying houses, utilities and hotels, a skill in which I was woefully deficient, so their accumulated fortunes in play as in real life were much greater than mine. But I loved rolling round my tongue the names of stations and well-known London streets like Fenchurch Street and Piccadilly which appeared on the board.

Another game in which I was more successful was Battleships. The aim was to try and sink your opponent's ships, which were represented by squares on paper, by guessing their position. The overtones of battle-engagements that the game implied made winning all the more satisfying. To sink enemy ships even in fantasy gave some feeling of control of events.

As we were now settled into some kind of routine, my aunt decided it was time I went to school again. The local primary school was housed in a bright modern building in the shape of a square. Along three of its sides were classrooms, and inside the square ran a corridor supported by pillars. This was open on one side to the prevailing winds and weather, since it was considered healthy for the children to have plenty of fresh Devon air in all seasons. In the middle of the building was a grassy space, and at the top end of it were the hall and the headmistress's room, into which we were shown by the school secretary.

The headmistress was a tall, formidable-looking lady. Sensing trouble, she cast a wary eye over me. After this inspection she handed me a piece of paper and a pencil and commanded: 'Write "I like living in Paignton!"'

I was not sure that I did, but thought I had better do as I was asked. By now my English was improved and I was able to write the sentence out correctly, taking particular care with the spelling of 'Paignton'. The headmistress noted my effort with

71

some surprise. She had evidently been told that the new pupil had little or no English. 'That's very good!' she said. This must have prompted her to put me in a class with children of my own age.

In the weeks to come, lessons floated by me in a fog of incomprehension. I was absorbing words and phrases, but contributing nothing myself. One day when the fog cleared a little, I heard the teacher say:

'Today we're going to learn about area. Now does anyone know what I mean by that?'

This rang an immediate bell with me, for hadn't I heard the grown-ups at home repeatedly saying: 'Must have an aerial – no good without an aerial'?

Triumphantly I put up my hand. The teacher, a tall, red-haired Welshman, flushed with pleasure at this unexpected intervention from the foreign pupil.

'Yes, Martha', he smiled encouragingly, 'what do we mean by area?'

'It's for wireless', I replied eagerly.

And the class fell about laughing.

To my recently acquired title of 'the refugee' was now added another: 'the evacuee'. I hated both heartily, wishing only to be a normal member of the class. To add to my embarrassment, my long German name of Immerdauer often caused a crisis at registration-time. A teacher who was not used to it would run rapidly down the list of names he or she could cope with, then go on to my first name, look puzzled, cough, start on the first two syllables, pause and finish with a version of the last part which could be 'dor' or 'door' or 'dar'. I resigned myself to accepting all these variations as the quickest way of getting on to something more interesting.

Hearing this strange name, some of my classmates decided I must be a German spy. They reckoned that the proper treatment for spies was to make their life as uncomfortable as possible. So three of them, of varying sizes and degrees of threat used to waylay me after school, chase me on the way home and if they caught me, trip me up and punch me. My solution to this problem was pragmatic: every day I took an umbrella with me to school and when my attackers got too close, I would beat them about the legs with it. There were difficulties in explaining to my foster mother why I needed an umbrella on perfectly fine days. Yet in spite of this, it never occurred to me to break that code of silence that stops children from telling adults about such incidents. Fortunately, though, whether because they were discouraged by my primitive form of self-defence or simply bored with following me, my assailants soon gave up and I was allowed to walk home in peace.

As my knowledge of English increased, I was able to make friends and join in all the activities of the class. We spent long afternoons in church halls while a school evacuated from London en masse made use of our buildings in a box-and-cox system. Here we did country-dancing, singing, painting and all kinds of creative pursuits. We wrote our own plays and performed them to a musical accompaniment by one of the boys who was a good pianist. We dressed up in costumes supplied by willing parents and mounted displays of our work. I enjoyed this haven of sanity, although at the back of my mind was always the question about what might be happening to my parents in war-torn Europe.

Gradually my learning difficulties at school eased. I had always been quick at arithmetic and I soon found I could cope with sums involving pounds, shillings and pence as well as the problems about bath-taps and men working in fields which were the staple of primary school mathematics. (I have some sympathy with the refugee boy who, when faced with one of these conundrums, reputedly sighed to his teacher: 'Missis, I wish I had your problems and you, mine!')

Nevertheless, arithmetic was the easiest of the hurdles I had to overcome. A more complex one was achieving fluency in a new language and understanding a new culture. I was desperate to learn English quickly because I hated not understanding what was going on around me. Also it seemed natural to me to speak more than one language because I had

had experience of my parents speaking Polish as well as German, of my father praying in Hebrew, and of my foster parents speaking Polish and Yiddish as well as English.

I know I had a strong German accent at first. I found the 'th' sound hard to reproduce as anything but 's'. Also my 'r' sound must have been guttural because I remember someone making fun of it when I pronounced the words 'scchratch' and 'bchruise' after I had had a fall. However, I have a good ear for nuances of sound, so it did not take me long to adapt my vowels and consonants to the English pattern. I cannot remember precisely when I shed my German accent, but it was some months after I arrived in England. To this day, when I tell people that I was born in Austria, they say: 'Oh, but you haven't got an accent!'

My vocabulary increased daily. I was delighted to find I could read again. In comics like the *Dandy*, for which I had a weekly standing order, I followed the adventures of Desperate Dan and other stock characters. Later, I progressed to the stories of Angela Brazil and L. M. Montgomery which I borrowed from the public library. By now I could manage to understand and enjoy the children's programmes broadcast by the BBC. Toytown and Uncle Mac were great favourites. I also loved the extracts from *Pickwick Papers* and the stories of Brer Rabbit our teacher read to us. I delighted in poetry and felt envious of pupils who were able to recite poems in front of the class. I would dearly have liked to do the same, but had no idea how to get access to such riches.

Soon I became fluent in English to the point where I stopped thinking in German. With straight brown hair, fair skin and small features, I was outwardly indistinguishable from my English classmates. Inside was another matter. I had the childish delusion that somehow other people knew what I knew, understood what it was like to be persecuted in Nazi Austria and forced to flee your country without your parents. At home there was indeed some awareness of what I had gone through. Being Jews, they knew about persecution, but I wonder what my English classmates made of me.

What had happened to me was so painful that it was quite beyond my powers to talk about it. There were hints of sympathy from my aunt and her friends, but I hated these and found them a burden rather than a comfort. I had no wish to be pitied by anyone. Incredible though this may seem, I never talked about my Austrian past or my real parents to my English school-friends. How much they had gathered about me from other people I have no idea, but they colluded with this silence either through tact or lack of curiosity. We chatted about day-to-day matters, made fun of the teachers and discussed who in the class was sweet on whom. For me the past was like a cupboard on which I firmly turned the key.

Sometimes I was invited to other children's houses. This put me in touch with the ritual of English tea; thin sandwiches, scones and cakes all served in a special order. Instinct told me not to take the most attractive pastry when there were not enough of these to go round. But returning hospitality was another problem. My friends, having no experience of fostering, assumed that my foster mother was my real mother. Calling her 'auntie' as I normally did, would have entailed long explanations, of which I was emotionally incapable. I dealt with this dilemma by not addressing my aunt directly. This imposed a severe strain on my already delicate equilibrium.

Then there were the questions: 'Are you High Church or Low Church?' I did not even know what this meant; nor do I remember what answer I gave. Whatever it was, it must have puzzled them, but they dropped the subject to my great relief. As Christmas was approaching, the mother of a friend I went to play with asked:

'What carols are you learning at school?'

'Good King Wenceslas' and 'The First Nowell', we replied.

To my surprise she knew them well and proceeded to play these tunes and some others on her piano. The only German carol I had remotely heard of was '*Stille Nacht*', so this extensive repertoire of religious songs was quite new to me. Such things were not talked about in the house my aunt shared with her cousins. However, in those troubled first months of the war they did manage to get hold of some small candles to celebrate Chanukah, the Jewish festival of lights which also occurs in December.

My aunt, a stickler for the proprieties, sent me to the Hebrew classes which were run on Sunday in the same school building I went to during the week. The teacher, who had the advantage of being a general subjects teacher as well, was a brisk and pleasant man. By making learning attractive, he increased my knowledge of the Jewish festivals and improved my ability to read the Hebrew prayers which are recited in the synagogue. Concurrently with this, I learned about the parables of Jesus in Scripture lessons in my primary school. To me, who loved all stories, they seemed interesting and their message unexceptionable. Nevertheless, I felt some guilt about listening to them because of the strong Jewish taboo against the New Testament. As there was no precedent for withdrawing children from the class for these lessons – I was the only Jewish child there – it was taken for granted that I would stay with the others. My aunt had more pressing things on her mind than to trouble herself with finding out exactly what I was being taught. The authorities had not caught up with this anomaly either. This was lucky for me, as being withdrawn would undoubtedly have increased my sense of alienation.

Once or twice my aunt had to go to London for a few days to make sure the house in Bow was intact. At these times I stayed with one of my schoolmates for company. She took me along to her Sunday school where we played boisterous games followed by a story and a Christian prayer. At home, by contrast, candles were always lit on Friday night and my aunt travelled some distance to get our meat-ration from the kosher butcher in Torquay.

These happenings went on in parallel. I kept them in separate compartments of my mind, telling my Christian friends nothing about my Jewish experiences or the Jewish adults about my Christian ones. Deep down I had a strong sense of identification with the Jewish tradition as a continuation of

part of my upbringing in Austria. Yet I found it hard to understand how the harmless and indeed, benevolent, extracts from
the New Testament we had read to us at school fitted in with
the vicious religious intolerance that prevailed in that country.

Integrating these conflicting strands of culture, language
and religion would have taxed the intellect of a mature
philosopher, let alone a nine-year-old child. In addition to this,
the Nazi experience had not been without its baleful effect.
Although I loved my parents deeply and my experiences of
living in the Jewish community were almost wholly positive, I
could not help the unconscious feeling that there was something wrong and shaming about being Jewish. Now, when I
recall the hideous caricatures of Jews even in the literature of a
relatively tolerant country like England – Fagin, Svengali and a
host of others – this no longer surprises me.

I felt embarrassed when my aunt talked to one of her friends
on the bus in Yiddish.

'And if French people talk in their language, nobody minds.
Why should you worry if I speak in Yiddish?' she would
counter with greater logic than I could muster on this delicate
subject. I could have wished for a mother in the mould of Mrs
Miniver complete with upper-class English accent instead of
this dumpy foreigner. I disliked it too, when some of her
relatives used expansive gestures in the street, which marked
them out as obviously different from the saturnine Devonians.
I was once reproached with passing one of these relatives with
a friend without acknowledging him. I felt ashamed of this act
of rejection afterwards, especially since, despite their alien
characteristics, my aunt and her relatives coped with the
demands war made on them, and their sons, and even
daughters, joined up when the call came. They for their part
had little understanding of how I felt, but they had not been
subjected to Nazi propaganda at an impressionable age.

Meanwhile to my surprise I was still getting letters from my
mother, although all official communication with Austria had
been cut off. She had a brother in Antwerp who forwarded her
letters to me and vice versa. She did her best to sound hopeful

about an eventual reunion and was guarded about telling me anything about the harassment she must undoubtedly have been suffering. I, in my turn, did my best to reassure her about my health and safety. Unfortunately these letters were not kept, so the only example I have of my parents' handwriting is my father's contribution to my autograph album.

What saved my sanity in those trying times was the stable routine of school and home. I owe much to my form-teacher and my foster parents for these. I loved learning: history, geography, nature study – all were grist to my mill. Literature, especially poetry, made a great appeal. I recall with pleasure the whole class reciting Alfred Noyes' 'The Highwayman' and identifying with the drama of the girl who warns her lover of danger with her death. There was also a host of creative activities, as I have already mentioned. I was pleased to be given a speaking part in a scene from *A Christmas Carol* that the class were rehearsing. The part may have been small – it was Mrs Cratchit – but I made sure my rendering of it was expressive. Our teacher, a musical Welshman, used to accompany our singing with gusto on the school piano. The songs he taught us – 'All through the night', 'Where e'er you walk' and a version of Handel's minuet from *Berenice* – were added to my store of remembered treasures.

I think of this as a period of relative happiness. Part of my mind, it is true, was weighed down with distressing memories and hedged about with inhibitions – things I could not express or allow myself to think about. Yet in spite of this, there was security in the long evenings as we sat round the fire roasting potatoes and knitting balaclava helmets for the Forces. However, this interlude was not to last much beyond Christmas. London was deceptively quiet. My uncle and Helen's husband were there. Naturally, their wives wanted to join them. So I said goodbye to my schoolmates and we set off for London, leaving the old couple who had elected to remain, to sell the furniture back to the auctioneers from whom they had bought it and to find rooms elsewhere.

When we arrived in London I noticed banks of sandbags

round official buildings, even more barrage balloons in the sky and batteries of anti-aircraft guns in many of the open spaces we passed on our way from the station. Bus-windows were covered with a greenish netting against flying glass, which made them look like aquariums. Posters showed someone tampering with one of these and a character called Billy Brown of London Town admonishing him with the words:

> I trust you'll pardon my correction –
> That stuff is there for your protection!

Merchant Street, which had so recently teemed with life, was now almost deserted. Most of the women and children had been evacuated to safer places, so that only a few men, compelled by their work to stay, and air raid wardens, were left. There were no ball-games in progress against the shelter wall. Undeterred, my aunt unpacked our belongings and reclaimed her domain with relief. She had not relished sharing a kitchen. My uncle had many practical skills, but cooking was not one of them. He had therefore been obliged to take up lodgings with a friend during our absence in Paignton. He too was glad to get back to his own bed and my aunt's cooking.

Most of the people my aunt knew were still evacuated, except for her friend Debbie who had refused to leave London. I remember her as a woman with a heavy body encased in voluminous overalls. She peered at you short-sightedly despite her thick lenses. Her air of imperturbability and her cheerful greeting "Ow you going, Millie – or Mary – or Martha?' made you feel instantly welcome. Her husband had died some years earlier, leaving her with a family of five children whom she had somehow managed to feed and clothe in the days before the Welfare State took care of such matters. They were now grown up and some were in the Forces.

Throughout the war Debbie literally kept open house. It was her boast that, like the Windmill Theatre, her front door never closed. In her tiny house in Mile End she accommodated some of her children and various lodgers. At the weekend her home became a meeting-place for relatives, friends and an assortment of young people invited by her children. These might include Polish soldiers on leave, Free French airmen and, later, Americans.

The living-room, despite its modest size and shabby furniture, was packed with people. Some sat on rickety chairs round a table, others formed little chatting groups in the corners of the room. At intervals, tea and sandwiches were provided by Debbie and her family. Food was strictly rationed, so it was understood that visitors would bring something to contribute to the general pool: a packet of tea, a few ounces of butter, a tin of sardines or a home-made cake. Near the bay window at the front end of the room was an ancient and far from well-tempered piano. On this the younger son of the house would thump out popular tunes with his right hand while caressing the bass keys at random with his left. The sound produced was more cheerful than harmonious, but who cared? The performance, despite its imperfections, helped to boost our morale. His younger sister, a curvaceous blonde, tapped her high heels to its rhythm and swung whatever eligible young man happened to be near into a quick-step or foxtrot in the tiny space kept clear of seated guests.

One evening, not long after our return to London, the air raid siren sounded. After many practice alerts and false alarms, we wondered whether this was genuine. Still, it seemed safer to take it seriously, so we grabbed our coats, some blankets and a torch and made our way to the air raid shelter. As we left the house, the night-sky was lit up with the criss-crossing beams of searchlights. In the street, other people, similarly equipped, were also hurrying in the direction of the shelter. We had hardly settled ourselves on the slatted benches with our blankets draped around us for warmth when we heard a succession of bangs which became ever louder and more violent. It was the anti-aircraft guns in action. To this was soon added the sound of aircraft with the staccato engine-noise that betrayed their German identity and then the crash and rumble of exploding bombs. I sat there transfixed with terror in that cacophony. It was as though malevolent gods were holding a firework party with reckless abandon. As the planes roared overhead, people held their breath and gripped each other's hands. Their lips moved in silent prayer that the next load would not fall on us. Eventually the thuds became fainter and then died away altogether. Finally the steady note of the all clear, so much more welcome than the wailing of the alert, released us from our prison. With a sigh of thankfulness for being still alive, we returned to our homes. These too had been spared from damage on this occasion, but the air was thick with the smell of discharged weaponry and the smoke of distant fires.

This experience was repeated the following night and the one after that. It became almost a matter of routine to go to the shelter armed with Thermos flasks and hot water bottles. As we sat there in the semi-darkness, we sang 'Pack up your Troubles', 'Tipperary' and 'The White Cliffs of Dover' – anything to keep up our spirits and drown out the noise of the guns and bombs. It soon became obvious to my aunt that she had chosen the wrong moment to return to London, so once more, with our belongings packed and the house locked up, we trailed back to Paddington Station. My uncle came with us for a short while, but soon had to leave again, to my aunt's great anxiety. Once more I found myself in a boarding-house. Then my aunt rented furnished rooms in another part of Paignton. These were later exchanged for unfurnished ones as she had her furniture brought down from London. We now had quite a pleasant flat in the top half of a house on the main road and seemed all set for a longer stay.

I returned to the same school I thought I had left for good some weeks earlier. As I now had a much better understanding of all the subjects, I was pleased to be back. To get there I had to make four half-mile trips each day, as lunch was not provided, but the exercise did me no harm. My classmates accepted my return without curiosity and invited me to join a 'secret society' whose purpose I forget. The initiation rite consisted of standing on tiptoe for five minutes, not too difficult a task. One of the activities of the society was to write a story a week for the entertainment of the other members. This I relished and so began my lifelong love affair with the English language. I know of no other that gives such a richness of vocabulary and subtlety of nuance. Its poetry and other literature have given me pleasure and provided some compensation for the loneliness of my life.

During this period of relative domestic stability, we were daily assaulted by disturbing news from the outside world. The German Panzer (tank) divisions were now on the move. The 'phony war' was over and the real war had begun. On the newsreels we saw frightened refugees pushing hand carts loaded with their belongings as they hurried to get away from a danger zone. They were often dive-bombed and machine-gunned by Heinkel aircraft. Belgium, where my uncle lived, was overrun and with it, the source of letters from my mother. In the newspapers, thick lines and arrows showed the German advance. Holland and Norway were swallowed up. Both had put up some valiant if hopeless resistance against an army superior in numbers and equipment. The greatest blow of all was the capitulation of France. We rejoiced at the number of British troops from the expeditionary force who were rescued from the beaches of Dunkirk by heroic little boats, but it was now frighteningly obvious that we were alone and facing an enemy armed to the teeth no more than twenty-five miles away across the narrow strip of Channel that now separated us.

For me this situation was terrifying. I studied the maps of the German advance with a mixture of fascination and despair. I could already foresee a repetition of my Austrian experience as the German invaders began to 'sort out' the Jews. Once more I was surprised, though not reassured, by the unexpected calm of the grown-ups. I imagined, probably correctly, that they could not conceptualise the terrors that were in store for them if Hitler were to conquer this country as he had already succeeded in conquering so many others. This was a strange role-reversal: for once I felt I was more knowledgeable than they were.

The official response to this dangerous situation, however, was a practical one. Single women without domestic responsibilities were drafted into munitions factories, railings and other non-essential metal objects were transmogrified into shells and older men joined the Home Guard. This motley collection of men later became a figure of fun in the television series *Dad's Army*, but in those days it was a defiant symbol of resistance. Posters exhorted us to 'Dig for victory'. We obeyed by growing potatoes, cabbages, peas and carrots in our back garden. Other posters proclaimed 'Your courage, your cheerfulness, your resolution will bring us victory!' There were also the famous speeches of Winston Churchill which acted like a brandy to fortify us and give us new heart. These were sometimes counteracted by gloom-merchants who purported to have secret information about the date of the German invasion, a date which changed with each succeeding month.

Meanwhile our daily life continued as normally as possible. Some foods were difficult to come by, but my aunt managed, by keeping her eyes open and spending a good deal of time in queues outside shops, to get a few scarce items such as onions or apples or whatever was temporarily in short supply. By this means we enjoyed a reasonably healthy diet. As fats and red meat were severely rationed, we ate more fish, brown bread and baked beans, which seemed a restricted diet at the time, but is now regarded as healthier than the high-protein meals we indulged in in the 1960s. To make the rations go further, there were recipes on the wireless for eggless cakes and jams made from unlikely ingredients such as marrows. We also supplemented what was available in the shops by helping ourselves from the larder of Nature. My canny country friends knew where to find mushrooms, watercress, elderberries and blackberries. The elderberries were made into wine and I was allowed to fill pastry-cases with the sugared blackberries before they went into the oven.

We lived almost next door to a cinema which was the cheapest and most popular form of entertainment apart from the wireless. Once, it is true, I was taken to the Torquay Pavilion by the wife of my Hebrew teacher to a performance of *Swan Lake*, which was enchanting. The outing was clouded for me, however, by my hostess's obvious dismay at the price of the tickets and her doubts whether she could afford them. It had been her idea to give me this treat after all! Another time my aunt and I were invited to a concert by the people in whose house we had once taken lodgings. Their daughter, a violinist, was playing a concerto. My aunt, not well up in what she called 'sympathy music', caused some discreet amusement by asking what instrument a concerto was.

But the regular entertainment was the cinema. In its all-embracing darkness, penetrated only by the illuminated 'Exit' sign above the side-doors and the occasional flash of an usherette's torch, you could forget your own troubles and vibrate instead to the problems of the celluloid characters on the screen. Here I saw a complete and not always suitable medley of films: there were funnies with Will Hay or Laurel and Hardy, thrillers that made your flesh creep, Westerns in which you could tell the hero by his white hat, dramas and musicals. Some showed Bette Davis or Joan Crawford grappling bravely with psychological hang-ups; others, glamorous girls making flower-patterns in tanks. Sex, under the strict discipline of the Hays Office was decorous: short kisses, no cleavages, no couples sharing a bed. From films I learned a little about the Hollywood techniques of courtship – the sidelong glances and provocative body-language – but they were of no immediate relevance. A few films, such as *Escape to Happiness*, gave tantalising glimpses of people fleeing from occupied countries. I could not express in words what longings these stirred up in me for some contact with a world from which I was now completely shut off, how I yearned to know what was really happening as distinct from the sanitised version I suspected we were being shown on the screen.

London, to my aunt's great relief, was now quiet again. Hitler had too much to do elsewhere. He had also switched his attention to other cities – among them Plymouth, not many miles from us. My uncle continued to work in London during the week and to travel down to Paignton by train at the weekend.

When the Blitz started, more relatives and friends had arrived in Devon, among them my aunt's sister and her niece. One friend had a daughter of about my age – ten or eleven – who stayed with us while her mother made a brief trip back home. Unlike me, Barbara had a comprehensive knowledge of 'the facts of life' which she insisted on sharing with me forthwith. I knew about babies and that something happened to you around the age I was approaching. Occasionally, if I felt off colour, when my aunt told her friends about this, they would ask: 'Is it you know what?'

'No, too young', she would reply with a knowing wink. My response was to turn my head away in scorn from these busybodies.

About how babies got in and out of women's tummies I was quite vague. Barbara changed all that.

'You know boys have got a thing?' I had seen my young cousins undressed, so I could say I did. What she then told me they did with this 'thing' seemed incredible and rather disgusting. Undaunted, Barbara continued to fill me in with explicit information about the sexual activities of some boys she knew. I did not relay this information to my aunt or anyone else.

The grown-ups, if they discussed sex, usually did so in confidential whispers, punctuated by anxious glances at the children in the other part of the room to see if they were listening. We pretended to be preoccupied of course. Looking back on it, their code of conduct seems severe. Husbands who strayed were condemned, but women who did so came in for the harshest criticism. One acquaintance whose affair had led to the birth of an illegitimate baby was castigated in the most vicious terms.

Although I kept one curious ear open for the strange revelations of the grown-ups, my real interest was elsewhere. I had caught up with the other pupils at school. Soon after I arrived in England, my aunt had shown me two buildings, one stately and imposing, and another, plain and more basic.

'This is where you go if you pass the scholarship', she said, pointing to the former.

'And this is where you go if you don't', she said as we skirted the latter.

These words meant little to me at the time, but I guessed there was some cachet in passing the eleven-plus exam. It was now more than a year since those early days. I was ten and three quarters and had gone up into the top class of Oldway Junior School with my peer-group. The scholarship examination, to be taken next spring, was now an important factor in our lessons as we continued practising the three Rs.

At this stage, arithmetic gave me no trouble at all: I was quick and accurate at the four rules, fractions, decimals, problems. There were also verbal reasoning tests in which you had to fill in gaps like 'toe is to foot as ———— is to hand'.

I whipped through those easily enough. The third note of that triad was 'composition'. Being an avid reader helped me to acquire a good vocabulary and accuracy in grammar and punctuation. In addition to this, our teacher gave us regular spelling-bees to enable us to cope with the vagaries of English spelling. This preparation did not take me into the realms of the utterly incomprehensible, such as 'Cholmondeley', pronounced 'Chumley', but I came to accept that in this strange English language the word pronounced 'ruff' was spelt 'rough' and the word pronounced 'bau' was spelt 'bough'. By the spring of 1941, the refugee who had sat in bewilderment at the back of the class regularly had her stories read out as examples of good writing. My friends accepted this without spite or envy. They had their strengths and triumphs too.

Discipline in that class was effective but crude. Most of the time our teacher jollied us along by keeping us busy. We learned the difference between the informal parts of the day when we were allowed to talk quietly as we painted or worked together on a project, and the more formal parts when we were supposed to listen in silence. If anyone flagrantly disobeyed the teacher they would first be warned. Then, if they took no notice, they would receive strokes on the palm of the hand with a ruler if they were girls or a 'dusting of the trousers' if they were boys. I can only remember having this punishment meted out to me once. The humiliation added to the stinging sensation in your palm made you very resentful for a few days. However, these forms of punishment were a last resort and on the whole, we bore no grudges.

There were strict rules in the playground too: once the handbell for the end of playtime was rung you had to stand stock-still until you were allowed to line up to get back to your classroom. One day, after the bell had been rung, I noticed that someone in front of me had dropped a handkerchief. On an impulse I took a step forward to pick it up and handed it to her. I was summoned to the teacher on duty for breaking the playground rule and my explanation was ignored. After the others had gone in, she marched me to the headmistress's office. There I repeated my story, insisting: 'I only picked up something the girl in front of me dropped !'

The head looked as though she believed me, but feeling, I suppose, that she had to make some bow in the direction of supporting a member of her staff, she went to a cupboard and took out what looked like a very small, thin walking-stick with a handle at one end. Grasping this, she gave me one not very hard blow on each palm. I was disgusted with her, not so much because of the pain, but because of the unfairness.

A pleasanter experience was the announcement of a competition which we were encouraged to enter. Despite the bad news from the fighting-front, a defiant Paignton had decided to hold a music festival. One category of this festival was verse-speaking, for which I entered. We were given a choice of poems to learn and recite. I chose Blake's 'The Tyger'. I knew nothing about Blake or his purpose in writing the poem, but something fierce and savage in its lines came across to me and I managed to convey this to the audience. I was overjoyed when I was declared the winner in my age-group, and have the certificate of merit still.

7 • *Grammar school girl*

From the outside world came the news of defeat after defeat as the Germans became the masters of virtually the whole of Europe. Official sources tried to soften these blows – a rout became a 'strategic withdrawal' – but no one was fooled by the heroic voices and euphemisms of the commentators in the media. There were stories of atrocities against anyone who resisted. Shootings and reprisals were not unfamiliar aspects of German behaviour to me. It seemed in those dark days that nothing would go right for us. As children we were unable to make a major contribution to the war effort, so we collected milk-bottle tops and got on with our schoolwork.

I had never had any great faith that I would see my parents again. This was partly realistic: I had heard and seen enough to convince me that Hitler would not hesitate to destroy Jewish people if he had a mind to do so. The precise methods and sheer scale of the horror that was being perpetrated in Europe I could not imagine, but I was not greatly optimistic about the chances of a reunion. My aunt did chat about this and sometimes I used to wonder how, in that unlikely event, the two women would get on – my mother with her pretensions to refinement and my aunt with her peasant directness. As for me, whom would I belong to? I heard later of the problems of a devout Christian who had been married twice and wondered which husband she would be with in heaven. I could have been in a similar dilemma, but I did not take the chances of such an outcome seriously. Part of me was desperately upset and worried about my parents. I felt guilty that they had saved me from direct suffering when they had been unable to do as much for themselves. Another part of me wrote them off as unhappily useless parents.

In my smaller world everyone was now talking about the scholarship examination which was looming nearer. From remarks made by my teacher it seemed that, barring accidents, I was certain to pass, so I turned over the pages of my test papers with confidence. As far as I remember, they held few mysteries. I had almost forgotten about the subject when, some months later, a letter arrived announcing that I had been awarded a scholarship to a grammar school. In my excitement I rushed to meet my teacher on what I knew to be his route to school. He congratulated me warmly and when I got to school I learned that another pupil, David, the boy who played the piano, had had a similar letter. The news apparently came out in batches, for every day during that week brought letters to about a dozen pupils in that class of thirty-plus, among them all my friends. What happened to the others, or how they felt about us trumpeting our success I did not question. All I knew was that my hard work had been duly rewarded and I savoured my first taste of justice with satisfaction.

Now I had to choose beween two grammar schools: Torquay and Totnes. I did so on a simple basis: Torquay Grammar School was three and a half miles from my home and Totnes twice as far. I had grave doubts whether with my allergy to travelling I could even manage the shorter journey. The longer one would have taxed my endurance too severely, so I chose the easier option. Even then on the homeward journey I often had to get off halfway after fighting desperately the urge to bring up my lunch. Unfortunately, unbeknown to me, my friends had all chosen Totnes. This meant that there were no familiar faces on the school bus when I boarded it in my navy gymslip, white blouse and school tie, with the obligatory velour hat with its ribbon in the school colours – red and navy.

There was another disappointment in store for me. Our teacher had told us that at the grammar school there would be two sorts of pupils: those whose parents could afford to pay for their fees and those like us who had earned our place by our own efforts. Something he said gave us the impression that in that brew we would be the ones who came out on top. When

I started school in September, great was my astonishment when I discovered that far from this being the case, the 'private' pupils considered themselves several cuts above us. They had had a previous year in the preparatory school and some of the teachers colluded with them in their good opinion of themselves by sycophantic remarks like 'Oh, weren't you in the prep school?' I was furious.

To add to my troubles, my aunt had kept me off school for the Jewish Holy Days of the New Year and the Day of Atonement, the most solemn festivals in the Jewish calendar. When I returned, I found that the other first years had been tested for their physical aptitudes and put into groups labelled A to D, A being for the potential athletes and D for the hopeless duds. The gym-teacher, after the briefest of looks at me, dismissed me with the words 'You'd better go into the D-group'. I was annoyed not merely at being classified but at not being given even a chance to show my real ability. In revenge I decided to make little effort at gym.

Nevertheless, in the other subjects I did well. History, geography, English, science and mathematics – I enjoyed them all and grasped their essentials without difficulty. For someone who had already mastered one foreign language, French was a walkover. I cannot say that I worked like a demon because it all came rather easily to me at this stage. I used to belt through my homework in odd moments between lessons, and it was my boast that in that first year I rarely had to do schoolwork at home.

Socially I was not having a good time. I missed my primary school teacher whose personal tuition was now replaced by a dozen others sweeping by like black bats in their academic gowns, and a form mistress whose duties seemed to end with taking the register and telling us which syllables to accent in her name. She did nothing to weld together a heterogeneous collection of children, nor did she notice the unhappiness of one little girl with a long German name. To counteract my feeling of loneliness I used to joke and clown about in break to make my presence felt. This did not impress many of the other children. Only gradually did I acquire some genuine respect for my academic achievements, but even then it was difficult to make real friends. None of the others lived near me and in any case having them home would have entailed explanations which I thought better avoided. I continued to see my old friends at weekends, but they had formed new alliances and loyalties which excluded me.

After we had had our end-of-year examinations, the powers-that-be decided to gather up all the girls who had done well in the tests into a special second form called 2X which the teachers archly dubbed 'two excellent'. I was flattered to be put into this class which made up a little for my social isolation. Towards the end of that year another verse-speaking competition, this time only for our school, was announced. I had got hold of a poem by Kipling called 'The Glory of the Garden' and decided to enter with this. The poem begins with the line

'Our England is a garden that is full of stately views'.

It is all a metaphor for English society and a strictly stratified one at that. Another line goes

'And some are hardly fit to trust with anything that grows'.

Its imagery of statues, stately homes, peacocks, was entirely outside my experience, but something in me responded to the idea of pride and hard work. I used my most scathing tones for the lines

'Our England is a garden and such gardens are not made

By saying "oh, how beautiful" and sitting in the shade'

and my tones of fervent approval for

'While some go out and start their working-lives

By grubbing weeds from gravel-paths with broken dinner-knives',

finishing with a grand crescendo

'And the glory of the garden it shall NEVER [pause] PASS AWAY!'

I was quite unaware of the unsuitability of such a nationalistic poem for a little foreigner. Instead I identified with the aspects that made sense to me. I suppose it showed how thoroughly I was being forced to retreat from my true origins and identity. Yet I had to have some mould into which I could pour my pent-up emotions and this was all that was available to me. For that recitation I won a prize – a basket of red and white cherries. No fruit has ever tasted so good.

It was now the winter of 1942. I knew little of the terrible atrocities that were being committed in Europe, but for the British forces, things were looking up. There were the heartening victories of Montgomery's army in the Libyan desert to lift our spirits at last. For the first time our newsreels showed the Germans tasting the sour cup of defeat as thousands of them were marched to captivity. The sound of the bagpipes accompanying the British march into Tobruk is one I shall never forget. My aunt's friend Debbie had a son-in-law in the Libyan desert who used to write to all of us between the battles. These letters came to us in miniature writing on microfilm to save space on the aircraft that flew in the mail. Dave had spent his embarkation leave with us in Paignton and he even remembered to write to me in those fraught times. I have one of his letters still. London had now been free of air raids for some months. Once again, my aunt decided to move back, this time away from the East End to a flat in Clapton where she had friends. At great expense her furniture was taken back to London and the flat in Paignton vacated. I left my school without many regrets.

Before I did so, the headmistress summoned me to her room. She wished me well in my new school in London and kissed me goodbye. I was taken aback by the warmth of this leave-taking. I am sure there was nothing sexual in it; perhaps she recognised in me, for all my faults, a young person putting up a tremendous fight for her sanity in a partly insane world.

* * *

We now moved to a house in north-east London built on a much more generous scale than the little Victorian villa in Merchant Street. It was set further back from the road and the rooms were of more spacious proportions. We rented the upper part and the owners of the house occupied the lower. This time there was an indoor toilet and a bathroom (shared). The lady of the house was a short, slightly built elderly woman. Her face was as flat as a disc, with small features, wrinkled skin over two bright red cheeks and eyes that beamed in perpetual good humour. My aunt, who was of a much more nervous and fiery temperament, found it impossible to quarrel with her. Mrs Gold, the landlady, had two children still living with her, a bachelor son and a single daughter who worked in a munitions factory. When she was on the night shift the daughter would put her wiry auburn hair into curlers underneath a turban scarf and set off for work dressed in warm trousers. On our frequent meetings on the stairs we would share a joke or a giggle, while her brother did an imaginary Fred Astaire tap dance on the landing. From time to time my aunt used to pop downstairs for a chat. It was like living in a jolly extended family.

One day, the son and daughter of the house asked me whether I would like to go with them to the local variety theatre – the Finsbury Park Empire. Of course I jumped at the idea, as such treats did not often come my way. The show included an act by Wilson, Keppel and Betty who brought their own sand on to the stage in a bucket and did a soft-shoe shuffle and comedy turn on this. But the star of the show – unbeknown to me – was the stripper, Phyllis Dixey. In those days, nudes were not allowed to move on the stage. To get round this regulation, Phyllis Dixey, after removing her clothes progressively, was left covered by an outsize ostrich-feather fan. This she delicately put aside for a few seconds as the lights flashed on and off, to reveal her nude body in various (still!) poses. It was not the most suitable entertainment for a thirteen-year-old girl, but I'm sure it was kindly meant.

After my uncle had cut and pieced together lino from our previous homes and the furniture was installed, I was ready to start school again. We received a letter from the education authorities, stating that I had been allocated a place at the

93

North-East London Emergency Secondary School for Girls which was housed in the building of the Dalston County School in Shacklewell Lane. One morning my aunt and I set out for this address. When we arrived, we were shown into the headmistress's office. Her first words to us, spoken in a strong Scottish accent were:

'Why have you come back to London to give the air-raid warrdens trrouble?'

I can't remember what answer, if any, my aunt made, but after these unpromising preliminaries, I was taken to a second-form classroom.

I now found myself in a strange environment. At Torquay there had been no great sense of academic pressure. The school, surrounded by spacious playing-fields, set great store by the successes of the various teams at netball, hockey and rounders, teams composed of the healthy daughters of local farmers, shopkeepers, clerks, etc. The strain on the brain was minimal, yet the atmosphere was orderly. The same could not be said here. There were groups of pupils from half a dozen different schools in north east London: Skinners', Clapton, Raynes, Owen's, Coborn and others. The majority of pupils from each of these schools was still evacuated, hence this arrangement for educating together the small number who had come back to London. The result was a mixture of warring tribes. It seemed to me as though all the ragamuffins of London were assembled here. There were frequent fights in the play-ground and even punch-ups between lessons with writhing bodies on the dusty floor of the classroom. One girl was cruelly mocked and scapegoated. In general the atmosphere was as unpleasant as any I have ever come across in a school.

Lessons were conducted in a half-hearted way by dispirited teachers. Latin lessons found only myself and one or two other girls participating. Each of these would start with the greeting from us: 'Salve, o magistra!' and the response from the teacher: 'Salvete, discipulae!' After this ceremonious beginning, most of the class switched to more interesting pursuits like writing notes or reading magazines under the desk. A few of us, who had no objection to learning Latin, read from the textbook stories from Roman history about Regulus, a man of honour, of Horatius who kept the bridge (defended the bridge over the Tiber singlehanded against the Etruscans) and of the combat of the Horatii and Curiatii. These tales, no doubt geared to the tastes of public-school boys, were of limited appeal even to my knowledge-hungry self, but I enjoyed learning new vocabulary, especially as it helped me to understand the derivations of many English words.

I remember the French teacher as a jolly, outgoing person who did make an effort to inject some enthusiasm into her lessons. We were amused by the way she could switch very easily from broadest Cockney to 'Mayfair refaned' according to the person she was addressing. Other teachers made liberal use of films in an effort to keep us quiet. I saw many films that term.

On my first morning, after the bell had rung for the end of the last lesson, there was a wild scramble out of the classroom. Wondering what this was about, I hurried out, following the last of the mob. I found myself in what was obviously a dining-room furnished on the model of a penitentiary. Here tables were pushed together to form long rows set in parallel across the width of the room. At the far end was a serving-table from which stretched a queue of pupils. There was a certain amount of jostling and pushing in that queue, then a rush to fill up the seats and avoid the end ones. I was soon to discover the reason: the two girls at the end of each table had the duty of collecting up all the plates and wiping the surfaces of the tables after the meal. True to the spirit that prevailed there, people tried to make sure that this chore fell to someone other than themselves.

The meal itself was English cooking at its most debased. School dinners at Torquay had been unexciting, but I was unprepared for this. The serving ladies slapped onto your plate an oval-shaped piece of leather with a fringe of yellow fat. I was told this was roast lamb. At other times there would be a brown gristly mass topped with potatoes called shepherd's pie or a darker oval shape accompanied by a soggy wedge, the two together known as roast beef and Yorkshire pudding. These were submerged in a thin brown liquid and accompanied by a dollop of greens which, owing to over-conscientious cooking, would have been more aptly described as 'browns'.

The portions were decided by the servers and we were not allowed to leave anything on our plates. Teachers who had turned a blind eye to most of the other abuses of civilised behaviour in that dining-room suddenly became strict on this matter. I tried every device I could think of to rid myself of this unappetising mess. I gave some to people who actually wanted it and dropped bits under the table or even, when desperate, into a paper bag. The second course was much more to my taste. I liked spotty dog, jam roly poly and custard-tart. Sometimes there was tapioca pudding which was known as 'frog's eyes', but for the most part I enjoyed these examples of English pudding. My aunt's skills in this direction were limited to a compote of fruit – apple or plum – so these sweets proved a welcome extension to her repertoire.

I was helped to survive in that environment by a plump, round-faced girl called Sheila. Guessing my origins from my German name, she had decided to take me under her wing. Her common sense and imperturbable temperament enabled her to bypass the aggression of the mob and our friendship shielded me from its worst excesses. Sheila was the first Jewish friend I had made in England. Her parents were second-generation immigrants from Poland and the atmosphere of their home was not dissimilar to my aunt's. Like her, they kept the dietary laws (that is, bought their meat at a kosher butcher's and did not mix meat and milk dishes or eat pig-meat) and celebrated the Jewish Holy Days. This spared me the need for the sort of explanations I would have had to make to Christian girls.

Sheila's mother was a thin, anxious lady who criticised her daughter constantly. Her remark when Sheila had committed some trivial error, 'only my Sheila ...', became a catch-phrase for me. Her father, by contrast, was a fat and jovial man. He had had a grammar-school education in that nursery of famous talents, Central Foundation School which had produced such intellectual giants as Professors Bronowski and Brodetsky. He himself had not pursued an academic path, but had retained a lively interest in politics and the arts. At Sheila's home I had my first taste of intelligent discussion and my first glimpse of the *New Statesman*. It was through her father that we were encouraged to go to the theatre – the first play we saw was *Arsenic and Old Lace* – and became enthusiastic fans of the New Theatre in St. Martin's Lane where later Laurence Olivier and Ralph Richardson performed the classics so brilliantly.

In the autumn of 1943, Hitler was preoccupied with his attack on Russia and London had been free of air raids for some time. Therefore it was considered safe to allow the evacuated schoolchildren to return. As the emergency school was wound up, pupils who belonged to Clapton, Skinners', Owen's, etc., returned to their own buildings and a contingent of girls who belonged to Dalston County School returned from Downham Market in Norfolk where they had been evacuated. With the girls came several members of staff and the real headmistress, as distinct from the acting head who had given us such a tart welcome.

Miss Griffith, the headmistress, was an unglamorous figure. She was close to retirement age and had straight, short hair and a severe style of dress. Nevertheless, as we discovered in our dealings with her, underneath that severe exterior lurked the traces of a sense of humour and some compassion. In a quiet way she set about restoring civilised behaviour in the school. Gone were the fights and disturbances, the films and stop-gap devices. It became obvious that the staff meant business. Although by today's standards some of the lessons were pedestrian chalk-and-talk affairs, there was a general sense of competence among the teachers and an expectation of work from the pupils. The only casualty of this change was the departure of Sheila to the John Howard School in Clapton, but we kept up our friendship in spite of this.

* * *

As my knowledge increased, the gap between myself and my aunt widened. I had drawn strength in my childhood from her stability and affection without realising it. Now, in my adolescence I accepted what she had given me without a great show of gratitude, as teenagers are apt to do. Instead, I became acutely aware of her intellectual shortcomings. She tended to live her life like an animal well-adapted to its environment. She knew how to furnish a home, to cook and make relationships. What was outside her control was of no interest to her and she never dealt in abstractions. This resulted in some strange mis-apprehensions. I remember her saying to me:

'I've been to every seaside.'

She then named half a dozen resorts beginning with Bourne-mouth and ending with Margate.

'But auntie, how could you have been?' was my sceptical response. I tried to explain to her that as England was an island, there were hundreds of seaside towns and villages and she couldn't possibly have been to them all.

'I've been to every seaside,' she insisted. 'Only Blackpool I haven't been to,' she added, conceding one exception.

Sensing my arrogant disapproval of her ignorance, she would say:

'You're clever in education, but I'm clever in common sense.'

There was more than a grain of truth in that assertion, a truth it has taken me a long time to acknowledge.

In some ways my aunt appeared to me as a strange mixture: when smartly dressed for an 'affair' (a celebration of some kind) with her naturally wavy hair set by the hairdresser and a cigarette in her mouth, she looked a picture of sophistication, but underneath this air of modernity she harboured some weird myths and superstitions: I was not allowed to cross knives, as that betokened a quarrel; if someone dropped a glove and you handed it to them they were not to say thank you, as this would break up the friendship; if she or I decided to sew a button onto my blouse without taking it off I would have to chew a piece of cotton, as sewing on a person without this precaution would sew away their brains. The foot of the bed was never allowed to face the door, as that was how the dead were placed. Also if someone paid you a compliment, she would go 'tu, tu, tu' in imitation of spitting, to ward off the evil eye. God was much in evidence in speech and letters. When a cousin of my aunt's wrote to give us his news, the page was peppered with BH, PG, and TG, his own shorthand for bless him/her, please God and thank God. For much of the time my aunt talked in a Yiddish vernacular whose sharpness I can only now appreciate. It was rich in curses and put-downs, but also full of proverbial wisdom.

Many of my foster parents' friends were people like themselves, immigrants who from extremely underprivileged beginnings had made decent though not affluent homes and done their best for their families. Most of them were strangers to book-learning and some of them totally illiterate, which put me into a peculiar position. As the only one with a ready pen, I was obliged to take on the role of scribe and whenever letters had to be written to this or that person or authority, my skills were pressed into service.

Perhaps the most bizarre use of these was made by the youngest sister of a friend of my aunt's. Sadie had come to this country from Poland as a teenager. She was now older, but still very pretty, nubile and warmly friendly. Her ready smile, trim figure, dainty silk blouses and click-clacking heels charmed everyone. She had recently met and, after a brief courtship, married, Bernard who was soon called up into the army. This created a problem, for Bernard, born and bred in this country and a loving husband, was eager to correspond with Sadie. She, however, had omitted to tell him that reading and writing were not among her accomplishments.

I was therefore deputed to be the amanuensis for Sadie's epistles to Bernard and also the reader of his letters to her. This had its complications. Not realising that his letters would be seen by any other eyes than those of his beloved, Bernard let rip with steamy descriptions of his enjoyment of their union. As a shy and inhibited thirteen-year-old I could not bring myself to read these aloud in full and so produced a working summary of this explicit passion. Nor was this all, for Sadie, loving and outgoing though she was in personal relationships, had no more idea of writing a love letter than the man in the moon. She would dictate to me:

'Dear Bernard,

I hope you're all right. I'm not too bad myself.'

And more in this vein. Imagining the disappointment of the ardent lover at receiving these dispiritingly cold letters, I decided that, just as I had toned his letters to her down, I would tone hers to him up and give them an altogether warmer flavour. 'Darling Bernard,' I would begin, etc, etc.

What happened after Bernard's demobilisation I never knew, nor whether my part in the story was ever discovered, but their marriage did survive.

* * *

I was emerging from the chrysalis of childhood into a troubled adolescence. However, at least one aspect of my life was satisfactory. I was doing extremely well at all my school subjects. Success in this field fulfilled both my need for intellectual exploration and my need to make my mark, but emotionally there were some great gaps in my life. I lacked the opportunity to talk to understanding adults about any subject at all, let alone the very disturbing fears and sadnesses that I was burying ever deeper. My aunt and uncle were efficient and loving providers of my basic needs, but there was no possibility of a meeting of minds. My uncle's topics of conversation were limited to the happenings on the road during his working day and I found my aunt's sagas about her rheumatism, her miscarriages and the price she had paid for apples to give me a good diet, less than fascinating. I often studied the labels of sauce-bottles in preference to listening to yet another recital of an oft-repeated tale.

The companionship of brothers and sisters was something that, as an only child, I had never known and did not realise I was missing. In the daytime the presence of my schoolmates made up for this lack to some extent, but evenings tended to be quiet with just my aunt, myself and the radio for company. (My uncle was out late working in his cab.) On some evenings my aunt, who was a sociable woman, did have friends in for a chat or a game of cards to break the solitude, but at other times I was left undisturbed to do my homework on the kitchen table while she quietly mended socks or played a game of patience.

For all of us, the radio was the central feature of our lives. We listened anxiously to bulletins from the war-fronts, took down recipes from Grandma Buggins and heeded the advice of the radio doctor. By courtesy of the BBC drama department I heard my first performance of *A Doll's House* and many other plays by Ibsen and Shaw. *ITMA*, the comedy programme with Tommy Handley, was the perfect antidote to gloom. I don't know how much my aunt understood of Handley's quick-fire wit, but the catch-phrases of stock characters like Mrs Mop ('Can I do you now, sir?') and the inebriated Colonel Chinstrap ('Drink – I don't mind if I do – ') kept me bubbling with laughter. The strokes of Big Ben, the peal of bells before the morning news programme and the sound of Lilli Bolero on the World Service were powerful symbols of the security and steadiness of purpose of the British people. I clung to them as to a lifeline.

I was beginning to think for myself and to question accepted ideas. Some of my aunt's seemed a strange mixture. She had the suspicious attitude to non-Jews of people brought up in the ghetto. Their view of the Christian world was limited to their experiences of representatives of that world who were close at hand. Living near the turn of the century among poverty-stricken non-Jews in the East End of London they would have come across a good deal of drunkenness. This they tended to generalise. They had also experienced the anti-Semitism which cuts across classes in British society and was as likely to surface in a sophisticate like Hilaire Belloc as in the labourer next door. Not being scholars, they did not have access to the thoughts of great British reformers like John Stuart Mill or the sympathetic writings of George Eliot to mitigate this. On the other hand, the Easter hymn of hate against the killers of Christ would be enough to strike horror into the minds of simple people who felt themselves, however irrationally, involved in this guilt. When told of some anti-Semitic remark or behaviour, my aunt's response 'They hate us' made me choke with fury. Of real persecution I had had more than my share, but that it was universal took away any rag of hope I had in the existence of fairness. I knew I had received generous praise and much kindness from my teachers, for some of whom I felt great affection, yet my aunt's words made me doubt the genuineness of their interest. Did they teach me merely because they had to do so? Would they rather have had a class that was without people like me? I never fully resolved this conflict which complicated further my view of the world. To compound this, my aunt and uncle had two Christian friends, former tenants from their house in Bow, with whom they had a warm and loving relationship, and my aunt was well in with shopkeepers in Paignton, none of whom were Jews.

I was being socialised into a confusing mishmash of English, Jewish and Polish ideas and standards. At school we were brought up on the hymns and prayers of the Church of England. I didn't know this at the time, but accepted morning assembly as part of the normal school day. As a concession to the large number of Jewish girls in the school, the hymns that were chosen for the most part omitted the name of Jesus. Most were paeons of praise to God which, though not part of the Jewish tradition, contained no specific Christian dogma. Some I found positively reassuring – like the lines

> We need not bid for cloistered cell
> Our neighbour and our works farewell.
> Nor strive to wind ourselves too high
> For sinful man beneath the sky.

That did much to allay my perpetual sense of guilt that I was not doing enough to improve the world! Others, like the beautiful Brother James' Air, to which I learned to sing a descant, derived from Old Testament psalms and caused no problems.

Occasionally there would be one with some references to Christian dogma which I barely understood, but felt guilty about. I wondered, was it right for me to sing 'ransomed, healed, restored, forgiven'? We Jewish girls compromised by keeping silent on these lines. One reading from Isaiah puzzled me for a different reason: it said (of the angels in the prophet's vision) 'with twain they covered their head'. What they were doing covering their head with string I couldn't imagine. It was not till years later that I discovered that 'twain' meant 'two'.

Later there was a change of policy. The staff felt they wanted some more specific Christian input, so on three days out of five, there were separate assemblies for Christian and Jewish girls. I can understand the reason for this change, but its result was divisive. The Christian girls, who were in the majority, had their assemblies in the hall, a room in the plain style of the 1930s, but yet with some aura of dignity. We, on the other hand, were banished to the gymnasium among the wallbars and climbing-ropes. The first thing that hit us as we entered was the lingering smell of sweat and rubber gymshoes. When all were present, a prefect read a psalm, followed by a recital of the Hebrew prayer of the Shema, 'Hear o Israel, the Lord our God, the Lord is one', by those of us who knew it, in unison. The mistress in charge often showed by her facial expression that she wished she were somewhere else, a sentiment we shared. We then had to wait for a signal in a kind of semaphore in the corridor outside from the Christian head-girl to the senior Jewish prefect that the other assembly had finished so that our filing-out would not disturb them. I can see now the difficulty of reconciling two such intractably opposed traditions, but to adolescent minds the message that came across was that to be Jewish was to be second-class.

There were also separate Scripture lessons for Christian and Jewish girls. Our lessons were taken by a member of staff who was said to be the daughter of an Anglican clergyman. She was a tall, thin lady with pointed features, pointed shoes and an upswept hairstyle. Her height and the glasses she wore on a

103

chain round her neck made her look formidable, but her manner was milder than her looks. She seemed to have an absorbing interest in the more esoteric rituals of the Jewish religion which in my experience were 'more honoured in the breach than the observance'. In response to her questions, information about these practices was supplied by members of the class more knowledgeable than I. I felt we were being studied as though we were some obscure Polynesian tribe and found this exchange embarrassing. It reinforced my dislike of what I considered the more primitive and irrational elements of my religion. Later we had Scripture lessons from a Jewish lady. Once again we practised reading Hebrew prayers whose meaning we only dimly understood and she chatted to us pleasantly about her life. I did not gain much spiritual enlightenment from those sessions, nor was there any attempt to explain our tradition to the Christian girls or vice versa.

*   *   *

At this time my memories of my early upbringing and of my parents were tightly locked away. I had now been in England for five years and my life in Vienna was taking on a dream-like character. I remembered my mother's face – my father's was already becoming hazy – and some of her mannerisms: the way she wrongly diphthongised some vowels at times – the only trace of her non-German origin. I remembered a few intimate words we had shared like my pet-name, 'Utchi'. This derived from 'Mutzi', the German word for 'pet' which she called me sometimes, but which I could not pronounce when I was very small. I remembered being told the story of how, as a toddler, I had strayed a few paces from my parents in the street. When a lady stopped me and asked me who I was, I apparently gave my name 'Utchi Immerdauer' and my full address, much to the lady's surprise. These memories made the tears flow, so I could not bear to bring them out of hiding too often. As for the actual country where I was born, that seemed to me as inaccessible as the moon. This was so in reality as well as in fantasy, for we were still at war with

Germany and its satellite, Austria. On the surface, it was as though I had shed my Austrian language and personality as a snake sheds its skin and had grown a protective English covering.

Although I had come to England in a party of children, after my arrival I had no contact with any of them. At one time there were two other girls who came from Vienna in another class at school, but they had come here with their parents. One was a pretty, pert girl who was popular with her classmates. When we met in the playground, her friends used to say to us 'Come on, talk German!' I refused this invitation on principle, as I had no wish to be a performing flea, and made a hasty retreat from her gang. The other girl, quieter and less well-favoured, lived not far from my house in Evering Road. We sometimes walked home together, but I did not dare to ask her about anything to do with Vienna or what had happened to make her father a sick man.

One day I was surprised, therefore, when out of the blue came a suggestion from my teachers: 'Would you like to take up German again?'

I had so far been learning French and Latin and they wondered whether I might like to add German to these languages. I agreed to this idea and was timetabled to have some lessons with the class that learned German instead of Latin. I discovered that of the words I had not used for so long only the stems remained, so that I had to relearn the case-endings and conjugations. I realised also how limited my vocabulary was compared with my English stock of words, but of course I was stepping back into the shoes of a nine-year-old child. After some early struggles I did manage to master the grammar and later to gain a distinction in the subject in the School Certificate examination. It was typical of those times that nobody made any attempt to explain the reasoning behind this imaginative idea of my teachers, but it enabled me later to join up some fragments of my broken links with the past.

The war was now entering a much more successful phase. America had been drawn in by the Japanese attack on Pearl

Harbor and Hitler's army, which at one point had almost reached the Ural mountains, was being pushed back by the determined Russian defenders. Leningrad had also resisted a bitter siege. In previous years, expressing hopes of a favourable outcome to the war had been like whistling in the dark, but now there was a real prospect of victory. All was set for the return of the Allied forces to Europe and there were slogans on walls shrilly demanding 'Second Front Now!' Hitler chose this time to launch his final act of aggression against London in a renewed bombing campaign. There were sporadic air raids, not as intense as before but menacing enough to life and property. My aunt prudently took rented rooms in Hitchin in Hertfordshire, a town we had stayed in during a school holiday. The arrangement was that we spent the week in London and retired to the safety of the countryside at the weekend.

I had recently joined a Zionist club which met at our synagogue every Sunday. I was fascinated by the chance of meeting new people – boys as well as girls – and learning about the pioneers who were building up the Jewish land of Palestine as it was then called. It was exhilarating to hear about some achievements by Jewish people. So far, in addition to the persecution I had suffered myself, I had picked up gruesome stories of the Spanish Inquisition and the expulsion of Jews from many countries in Europe. Here at last was something positive, something to be proud of. We also learned songs and dances – much more fun than the monotonous chanting of the Saturday morning religious Service. The move to Hitchin meant that I could not get to this club. One weekend I begged to be allowed to stay in London with the Gold family so that I would not miss yet another meeting, but my aunt was adamant. No, I was not to go. Next day we had a telegram to say that our house in Evering Road had been hit by a bomb. There was some justification for my aunt's 'I told you so!'

When we returned to London to inspect the damage, we discovered that the Gold family had been in the shelter when the bomb struck. They were shaken but unhurt. The house looked a sad mess. There were broken glass, bricks, dust and rubble everywhere. The roof was half off, the walls buckled and chunks of plaster had been ripped off by the blast. Strangely enough, our furniture was virtually undamaged except for one of the monstrous vases which had decorated my aunt's sideboard and now lay in smithereens. After commiserating with the Golds, who went to stay with their married daughter, my foster parents arranged to have our furniture stored till a new London flat could be found. Home now became the rooms in Hitchin which had been our temporary refuge.

After this, my aunt did her best to persuade me to change to a local school. This time I dug in my heels. I had started a course leading to School Certificate in which I was taking eight subjects. I was doing well and was anxious to make a good showing in the examination. I argued that a change of school at this crucial time and probable changes of syllabus would put paid to my chances. Eventually a compromise was agreed: I was allowed to go to school in London in the daytime provided that I returned to Hitchin at night, which was the time when the bombers were most active. This meant getting up at 6 am in an unheated house on cold mornings. I used to shiver as my aunt put the kettle on for a quick wash and hasty breakfast. Then I would set off alone in the grey morning light across the recreation-ground, past the bacon-factory that sent its malodorous smell wafting across the park and into the dimly lit station to catch the London train. With my school-case on my lap, I sat there drowsily as the train stopped at familiar stations – Knebworth, Hatfield, Welwyn Garden City – till finally I heard the adenoidal cry of the guard: 'King's Croass auney!'

On one occasion I did fall asleep to find myself at the end of the line and had to retrace my steps, but usually I managed to shake myself awake at Finsbury Park, and then two more bus rides would take me to school, often late for assembly.

This arrangement, though physically tiring, did allow me an uninterrupted run-up to School Certificate. What I resented was not being able to see my friends out of school hours. They still had homes to go to and their parents had decided to stick it out in London for the time being, so they were able to socialise in a way which was impossible for me. My day consisted of travelling, school, more travelling and study - all work and no play. Compared with what young Jewish people on the Continent were going through, this now seems a very minor frustration, but I did not think so at the time.

There was also a lighter side to my journeys. Often there were American soldiers on the train. With their smart uniforms and the interesting accents we had grown accustomed to from the films, they were very attractive to us girls. By now I was wearing my hair in the fashionable style of the time with curls sweeping up from my forehead. This made me look quite grown-up. On one of my journeys to Hitchin my aunt was with me, but as the train was crowded, we could not get seats together. Next to me sat a handsome American who began to engage me in conversation. Flattered, I chatted to him for a while. He told me a little about himself and asked where I lived. Meanwhile from the opposite side of the compartment my aunt had been making disapproving faces which I pretended not to notice. She pursed her lips, shook her head, winked – all to no avail. Finally, unable to contain herself any longer, she hissed audibly in the direction of the American: 'She's only fourteen!' Our conversation died and he got off the train soon afterwards. I stayed on it with a baleful glare at my aunt for her spoiling tactics. Had she but realised it, I was far too immature to make any real relationships with strangers, so she could have spared herself some agony.

By this time, the wished-for Second Front had been opened. We followed with mounting hope the reports of the landings at Dieppe and other places and marvelled at the contraptions that had made them possible: among them a pipeline under the ocean (PLUTO), and a floating harbour (Mulberry). There were heartening successes as towns and villages in France were liberated from German occupation and pictures of tearful local people greeting the Allied soldiers with flowers and presents. At other times there was news of setbacks in areas where the Germans had chosen to make a desperate stand. We lived in a constant state of suspense and excitement.

Hitler then threw his last weapon into the fight against British civilians, the V1 flying bomb or doodlebug. This came to us as a complete surprise, as it was quite different from the patterns of air raids we had endured so far. As you were walking in the street you would hear the air raid siren. You would then detect the sound of an aircraft, distant at first but getting nearer and nearer. As the engine spluttered overhead, you held your breath and prayed it would go a little further. Suddenly it would cut out and you would brace yourself. A few seconds later there would be an almighty crash as the plane and its explosives hit the ground, not, if you were lucky, close enough to injure you. As these planes were pilotless, they did not need the protection of darkness, so now there were as many attacks by day as by night. This made nonsense of our arrangement for seeking safety in Hitchin at night, for no time was now safe. Often, on my way to school, I would have to duck into a doorway and pray that the horror in the sky would pass over me. At school, lessons were frequently interrupted by air raid warnings. This meant scuttling down to a part of the building which was reinforced against blast. To these viciously indiscriminate attacks by V1s were later added the even more sinister V2s – rockets which fell out of the sky with no warning at all, causing great loss of life. Despite these hazards, morale was high because we were obviously winning the war.

In fact, this last ordeal of the civilian population was soon to end as the advancing Allied armies overran the bases from which the V1s and V2s had been launched against London. To our enormous relief, we were safe from further attack. There was now no reason for staying on in our cramped and inconvenient quarters in Hitchin. The problem for my foster parents was that, with much of the housing-stock destroyed, flats in London were as hard to come by as pork in Golders Green. Resourceful as ever, my aunt managed, through the good offices of a friend, to find us a place to live at the Bakers' Arms in Leyton. It was above a shop that sold electrical goods and fittings. You entered it via a door at the side of the shop from which a dark staircase led to the upper floor. The shop, when open, blared out an unending stream of amplified music, so that we greeted closing time with relief. The rooms themselves were gloomy, with dark wallpaper that had seen better days, chipped brown paint and a bath that had a perpetual rim of grime, as it was used by the landlord to wash his dusty lampshades without a by-your-leave. Our furniture, now out of store, looked oddly forlorn there. Nevertheless, we were lucky to have a flat in London at all and it meant that I no longer had to get up at the crack of dawn to get to school.

Now came an important development in my life. I had grown from childhood to adolescence with simple though stable people, but completely cut off from my real parents and relations and the land of my birth. My foster parents had also come to this country as immigrants. They had never been back to Poland and seemed to have had no wish to do so. Nevertheless, they did have sisters and cousins in England with whom old family ties could be kept up. I could not feel a part of this network of kinship. When from time to time my foster parents' friends and relations invited us to their weddings and barmitzvahs, I always felt the onlooker at their feasts. A new dress and curled hairstyle in no way diminished my sense of being at the edge of things while the greetings, bawdy jokes and family reminiscences buzzed and lapped around me.

I had had similar feelings while an evacuee in Paignton. On my way home from school I used to pass handsome houses with well-kept hedges and front lawns. There was an air of permanence and seemliness about them, qualities so absent from my life. I used to walk past these smug citadels with their notices 'No hawkers, circulars' (who or what was a hawker, I wondered and what was a circular?) and feel they were giving me the message 'Keep out! You don't belong here!'

Inside I imagined was a privileged world which had no room for flotsam like me. Sometimes a passer by, usually a man, seeing me walk along sad and bemused, would call out 'Cheer up!' and I would do my best to smile.

* * *

Out of the blue came a letter addressed to me with a Palestine postmark. Who could it be from? To my great surprise it was from my father's sister. She had somehow managed to find my address and to get in touch with me. This came as a complete shock. In my other life my father had told me about my aunt Irene who had emigrated to Palestine, so here was the proof that the distant world of my childhood really existed! It was a small breach in the dyke of my isolation.

My aunt enquired about my health and well-being, but made no mention of my parents. She enclosed a photograph of herself and her husband taken outside their shoe-shop in Allenby Road, Tel-Aviv. I recognised the address from letters received by my father. There was also a picture of their son, an earnest-looking young man in the uniform of the British Army with three stripes on his sleeve. Here at last was something to be proud of! Real flesh-and-blood relatives, one of them even fighting in the war. I hardly knew how to express my joy at this unexpected discovery.

By now we had endured more than five years of war. We had put up with some food shortages: bananas were a thing of the past and for sweets we either tried to make our own toffees with dubious recipes passed round at school or rushed to buy the lemonade powder that was on offer in one local shop. Still, these were not serious health hazards. There were other inconveniences: clothes rationing meant that everything had to be made to last – make-do-and-mend was much in evidence – and in the home nothing was renewed or redecorated. Worse than this, London was full of destroyed or damaged buildings. After the rubble had been cleared away from a bomb-site what remained was often the end wall of a house with the fireplace and wallpaper exposed to public view. There was something obscene about this uninvited glimpse into what had been the privacy of someone's home.

111

Although there had been terrible casualties among the air-crews who manned the Spitfires that engaged the German bombers and among the soldiers who fought in the north African campaign, most of the sons of my aunt's friends were lucky enough to survive: her cousins' sons in the RAF had managed to avoid being shot down and Debbie's son-in-law, home at last from the Libyan desert and the Italian campaign, was given a hero's welcome. The neighbours stretched bunting across the narrow Mile End street to which he returned for a well-earned leave. My uncle had been too old to be called up, but had had some close shaves while working in the West End during air-raids. However, many families were less lucky. I remember a girl in my class coming to school red-eyed after her parents had received a telegram from the Air Ministry informing them that their son had been killed in action. Typically for those times, as far as I know nothing was said to her either by the staff or the girls. The stiff upper lip prevailed. As for the people at home who had been either too young or too old to serve, we were shabby and weary, but hopeful now that the end was in sight.

At this point came a further move. My aunt had found better accommodation in Clapton and once more we packed up our belongings. Once again my uncle fitted the old lino, which was beginning to resemble a jigsaw pattern, to yet another kitchen floor. I realise now that in the war years I had lived in seven different flats, not counting temporary stays in boarding-houses. The longest time I had stayed in one place was in the two years between the winter of 1940 and that of 1942. I cannot account completely for these gypsy wanderings. My aunt was not by nature restless and irresponsible and some of the moves were out of necessity, but I don't think she realised the effect they had on me. Fortunately for my sanity, the continued concern and affection of my foster parents was at least one constant I could rely on.

The 'new' flat was again the top half of a house, this time a rather grand one sold by its previous owners because of war-damage. This was now repaired. The attic had been a billiard-room in better days and what became our living-room boasted some imitation oak panelling. The kitchen, by modern standards, was ill-equipped, the only fitting being a Butler sink with a cold tap and a cupboard underneath. The living-room which once again contained the 'best' furniture, remarkably unscathed from its many peregrinations, was spacious, as were our bedrooms. There had been central heating, to which the ubiquitous radiators bore witness, but the landlady who lived downstairs declared the boiler to be broken, so the system was never used. Food was kept in a tiled well in one of the extensive cellars or in a safe in part of the hall outside our kitchen. In winter, the temperature of this hall made refrigeration unnecessary. The bathroom, being unheated, was more symbolic than practical for six months of the year, but once a week a geyser was prodded into action by the people downstairs and we took it in turns to have our regulation six inches of hot bath-water.

My room was again sparsely furnished with the same items that had been in place in Merchant Street. Some pretty chintz curtains and a flounced bedspread to match were the only concessions to my budding femininity. There was now also a folding card-table which did duty for a bed-table and on this stood a lamp which was a great improvement on the torch with which I had had to read in bed in secret in my tenderer years. What redeemed the room, which was at the top of the house, was a magnificent view of the river Lea. From my window I could see its grassy banks and islands and the vertical forms of sawmills and other factories on the further side. Often there were boats gliding past and occasionally the hoot of a ship's siren broke the silence. On misty days it was a scene of mystery and romance, far removed from the dreary surroundings I had lived in so far.

The owner of the house was a thin, ineffectual man, but his wife, a plump figure dressed in shapeless skirts and jumpers, made up for this. She would mount the stairs to our flat, munching an apple and settle down for an hour's gossip with my aunt. When an urgent message had to be given, she would trumpet up the stairs 'Missus Gee!' (her name for my aunt) in a volume fit to wake the dead. My aunt, for her part, if her washing was interrupted because someone was using the tap downstairs, would stamp her foot like a little Rumpelstiltskin – enough to shake the ceiling below while uttering a piercing cry of 'Vauter!' which resulted in swift compliance with her imperious demands.

* * *

I now had a much easier journey to school. There I found friendship and intellectual stimulation, but little understanding of my peculiar emotional problems. Counselling or therapy of any kind was not available to ordinary mortals – no one in my circle had even heard of Freud – so I swallowed hard and made the most of what was on offer. What was on offer was British culture, spread over us like a seamless garment without regard for our own origins or backgrounds. Foreigners did not figure much in our reading-matter and geography consisted of a study of the British Isles, the Commonwealth and North and South America. Europe, Africa and Asia were not part of the scheme of things. History did include European events, which was a welcome extension of this narrow focus. I found the politics of the nineteenth century, our set period for School Certificate, fascinating.

Science gave explanations of how mirrors, lenses, cameras and torches worked – all very useful – and biology satisfied my curiosity about the make-up of living things. A rudimentary form of sex education followed a study of the male and female reproductive systems – in section. After we had done our drawings and duly labelled them, our teacher called out:

'Gather round, girls!'

When we had bunched around her desk, she announced in confidential tones:

'Now, girls, if you're out with a man, don't let him give you strong drink!'

Domestic Science was my least favourite subject. Needlework began with darning and patching and progressed to the making of a pair of navy blue gym-knickers. When I was first evacuated I had begged to be given tray-cloths and silks so that I could imitate in a small way the beautiful embroidered cloths I saw one of my aunt's cousins making. I still have some of these, painstakingly stitched and with delicate colour schemes, but there was nothing appealing in the garments we were expected to make in our needlework lessons. What little interest I started with was soon killed off by the demand that I unpick any seam which had the least imperfection, so that there never seemed an end to this dreary labour. I expressed my frustration when asked to make a bag by sewing up all four sides and was regarded by the teacher as the dunce of the class.

Cookery was the other subject I disliked. Early in the war I had enjoyed helping my aunt bake. She had allowed me to beat cake-mixtures and fill pastry-cases, but when I asked to be allowed to make a dish myself, she refused to let me in case I wasted scarce rations. After this, I lost interest and left her in undisputed charge of her domain, even taking a perverse delight in my ignorance of basic processes. Once at school we were asked to boil an egg. I took an egg and put it in a saucepan on the gas. When the resultant smell caused the teacher to call out:

'What stupid person has put an egg on without water?'
I realised it was me. Somehow my pastry was never light enough and my puddings never a perfect shape. I think some of this clumsiness was contrived, but I suppose being a model pupil in most other lessons meant I had to have some outlet for my rebellious instincts. In the fourth form we had to choose between Domestic Science and Latin. Thankfully I chose the latter.

As my interest in literature deepened, I continued to enjoy my English lessons. I had graduated in my private reading from the schoolgirl stories of Angela Brazil to the novels of Charlotte Brontë. When it came to class readers, little concession was made to our age or interests: Milton's 'Paradise Lost' and the essays of Addison and Steele were far above our heads, especially as no attempt was made to set them in their context. Also, after enduring the London Blitz, it was not easy for us to empathise with the desperate problems of the ladies in Mrs Gaskell's *Cranford* about how to eat oranges with propriety. Our teacher's chuckles were matched only by bewilderment on our part. However, the wit and verve of Jane Austen found a warmer response and I loved the poetry we were introduced to, ranging from Shakespeare sonnets to Gray's Elegy and Wordsworth's 'Tintern Abbey'. They put me in touch with a mood of thoughtful melancholy – part of 'the still, sad music of humanity' and a love of Nature far removed from the 'stormy clamour of wild war music' which dominated our real world.

8 · *The end of the war*

It was now 1945. The Russians were pushing westwards towards the Oder river and the British, American and Commonwealth forces were advancing deep into Germany. It was obvious that the Germans could not hold out much longer against their combined strength. It seemed a long time from the days when we had been alone and vulnerable, expecting to be invaded at any moment. The stubborn resistance of the British people, spurred on by the speeches of Winston Churchill, had now brought victory within sight. 'Unconditional surrender' was the new watchword and it was clear that the foulest régime the world has known was in for a humiliating defeat.

In my heart of hearts I both longed for and dreaded the end of the war, since I felt it was bound to confirm what I had feared all along: that I would never see my parents again. I had a deep sense of foreboding, nourished by my experiences of the Nazis and the scraps of information that had come my way, that there would be no happy ending to my story, though I had no idea yet of the scale of the horror that had been perpetrated on the Jewish communities of Europe.

School assemblies, which had included sermons and stories designed to stiffen our fighting spirit, now took on a gentler tone. We prayed for the safety of our soldiers, sailors, airmen and nurses and were exhilarated by their successes, but there was a feeling that such a conflict must not be allowed to happen again. Some of the hymns like

> O brother Man
> Fold to thy heart thy brother

and

117

> These things shall be
> A loftier race
> Than e'er the world has known
> Shall rise

chimed in with our youthful idealism and echoed the thought that there must be better ways of resolving disputes than the bloody enterprise we had been engaged in for nearly six years, inevitable though it had been in dealing with a megalomaniac like Hitler.

With the end of the war in sight, the question of what had happened to my parents, from whom I had had no word for five years, forced itself on my consciousness. I was now fifteen years old and very different in mind and body from the nine-year-old child who had tumbled into the arms of a compassionate foster mother. So much had happened, so much experience had been compressed into those five and a half years of exile from my real family, that there was little resemblance between the Martha of 1939 and of 1945. True, I could still speak some German, though with difficulty, and I had a few photographs and relics of my previous life, as well as some memories of my parents and school-friends, now growing hazy with the help of some determined repression. My early childhood was as remote to me then as an image caught between sleep and waking. I dared not contemplate it for too long for fear that the carefully built structure of my relationship with my foster parents and my success at school would tumble in ruins and shatter my precarious sanity.

In fact I had 'forgotten' an incident which occurred in the early spring of 1940 when I was ten years old, and even continued to do so while writing this account. It now comes back to me in all its horror. I received an official-looking letter from the Red Cross addressed to me. When I opened it, it said that my mother had been informed of the death of her husband. My aunt found me sobbing hysterically and, unable to read the letter herself, demanded to know the cause of my outburst of grief. When I told her, she insisted: 'No, it's not true!'

I knew this for a false and foolish reassurance, yet such is one's desire not to believe the worst, that I was half persuaded by her denials. To add to my confusion, I received a last letter from my mother. She spoke about my father as though he was indeed still alive. Caught between these two traps, I did my best to bury the whole incident. However, it strengthened my feeling that I would never see my father again.

* * *

Around this time, as the British forces were pushing further into Germany, there came news that they had liberated a camp called Belsen and that a film had been made of this camp which was to be shown in every cinema in London. I went to our local cinema with two friends, expecting to see film of people who had been badly treated, but the actual reality was beyond my worst nightmares. The piles of naked corpses devoid of flesh, the skeletal figures, scarcely able to walk, poking about for food among the filth, and the sick and dying, whose emaciated features and haunting eyes told a story of unspeakable suffering, made an impression I shall never forget. So did the pictures of the well-fed guards looking quite unrepentant at the evidence of their fiendish cruelty. I sat there in the darkened cinema crying silently, but not daring to give vent to my anguish. When the film was over, I dried my eyes surreptitiously and neither I nor my friends said a word.

That there were some survivors of the concentration camps I knew, but not how many or whether any members of my family were among them. My foster parents made enquiries through the Red Cross which confirmed my belief that my parents were dead. Exactly how or where they had been killed I have yet to find out, but it was felt at the time that there was little point in pursuing the subject, so it was left in abeyance for more than forty years.

My status as a teenage refugee was ambiguous. I learned later that I had had an official guardian called Lord Gorrell. Who he was and what he was like I had no idea, as this relationship was, as far as I know, a mere legal formality. Who did

I belong to then? I could not bear the thought of being an orphan. I had read about such children in books and knew them to be objects of pity. The very word made me shudder. On the other hand, I was a little old to be adopted by my foster parents and by then I had the feeling that, kind though they were, I was not of their kind. By tacit agreement, we continued our relationship on the old basis without legal backing.

The scheme for bringing refugee children to England had been drawn up in haste after *Kristallnacht*, and the war, with so many people scattered by evacuation, had made it difficult to keep track of these refugees. I had heard of unsuccessful placements among friends of my aunt, which did not surprise me, as I could imagine the problems involved. There had been no time to match the children to the foster parents – it was a case of any port in a storm – so small wonder that there was friction. Now that the war was nearly over, I did receive a visit from a lady from some welfare organisation. She came up the stairs to our kitchen, swept her eyes over the room to see if it was clean and tidy (it was), peered at me over her glasses to see whether I looked healthy and well-dressed (I did), commented (favourably) on my modern hairstyle, said a few words to my aunt and took her leave. She made no attempt to speak to me in private or to probe further into the situation I was in.

For my aunt, having a child to look after was the fulfilment she had craved. I do believe that, despite the undoubted stresses of the war and the adult responsibilities she had had to carry, the years of my childhood in England were a happy time for her. For me, they were more complicated. Having two sets of parents so different from each other and being brought up in so many contradictory cultures made life extremely difficult for me. Yet considering the circumstances in which I had been forced to leave my parents and the traumatic experiences I had already had in Austria, as well as the accurate knowledge I had of the German threat to our lives, I had a good deal to be thankful for during my early years in this country.

This halcyon period could not last into my adolescence. From remarks she let drop, I think my aunt had a rosy picture of motherhood with an obedient child as a perpetual companion – a cross between Lord Fauntleroy and Goody Two Shoes. Such unrealistic expectations were doomed to be disappointed. With so many bottled-up emotions it was no wonder that I developed a difficult personality, so that arguments arose over large and small matters. Her narrow and dogmatic ideas often clashed with mine, producing noisy outbursts from me which, as they met her volatile response, caused some notable explosions. For me there was a wild enjoyment in these slanging matches. They gave me the chance to pour out words and phrases with an eloquence my aunt could not match. My verbal pyrotechnics were a kind of play-outlet as much as an expression of disagreement with my aunt. This she could not understand. It never occurred to her that perfectly normal teenagers were sometimes bumptious and unpleasant to their parents and the 'appreciation and respect' she frequently claimed as her due were rare commodities among adolescents. When she was thoroughly wound up, she would shout at me:

'You wouldn't do this if I were your real mother!'

I could find no answer to this unfair charge.

This would occasionally be followed by the threat

'I'll report you to the Bloomsbury House!'

Sometimes when she had gone too far, I wondered whether I would not be better off in some institution where I would at least find rational people. But another part of me clung desperately to my place in an individual family, however imperfect.

Despite these set-tos, I know that my foster parents loved me. My aunt would express this crudely but touchingly by saying: 'I love you as though you were from my own belly.'

I loved them too despite the friction. In fact, my uncle, being a placid and peace-loving man, kept aloof from these conflicts. Sometimes, as he detected the onset of a fracas, he would murmur to me before leaving the house 'Be nice to Auntie!' and I would make an effort to please him. I doubt whether he could have done much to mitigate my aunt's excesses, as she was the dominant character in the household and he probably felt he had enough to do to earn his living on the streets of London. Although he was not able to intervene effectively on my behalf, his affection for me never wavered. Nor did he ever overstep the mark of what was permissible in our relationship as I grew to young womanhood. For his integrity and unfailing courtesy I owe him a good deal.

* * *

The long-expected end of the war brought relief that our protracted ordeal was over, though many families had reason to mourn as well as to rejoice. When the news of the German surrender was announced on the radio, my aunt and I hugged each other deliriously and hung a Union Jack, using a broom as flagpole, from our front room. Next day people literally danced in the street. Strangers embraced each other. Sailors, soldiers and airmen were swept into the arms of the bolder girls and their cheeks left plastered with lipstick from their kisses. Everywhere members of the armed forces were fêted and cheered. My friend Sheila and I joined the dense crowd that was converging on Buckingham Palace for a glimpse of the King and Queen and Winston Churchill. Squeezed together with thousands of other people, we could hardly make out the tiny figures on the distant balcony, but we were able to share in that profound upsurge of emotion that bound us all together. Later that week people celebrated with street-parties, bunting and music. Pianos and anything that could make a joyful sound were dragged out into the street to add to the noisy jubilation.

True, there was still another war going on in the East, but that affected us less personally than the war in Europe. The repercussions of its dramatic ending by the dropping of nuclear bombs on Japanese cities were not foreseen at the time. Of the movement of refugees across Europe and the scale of the deportations I had no idea. I don't believe they received a great deal of coverage in the newspapers that were available to me (my uncle took the *Daily Herald*) or if they did, I must have skipped those pages. That part of my life was so dead to me, along with the characters in that now-distant drama, that I shut such information out of my conscious mind as far as possible. All the details of the Nazi villainy were not generally known as yet except by scholars making a study of them. My aunt and uncle, being practical people unused to introspection and research, could see no point in such profitless knowledge. To me the whole subject was so painful that to delve into it would have strained my adolescent frame beyond endurance. It was left as a dark pit at the back of my mind for whose entrance I fashioned a cover of forgetfulness, a cover I dared not lift for many years.

With the war over and my parents' death a certainty, I settled down to make the best of my situation. This meant putting most of my energy into my school-work. Here there was a great deal to enjoy and I took part eagerly in all the activities that were on offer. My flair for bandying words and my newly discovered interest in current affairs found an outlet in the debating society. The *cercle français* taught me jolly songs like 'Auprès de ma Blonde' and 'Alouette', and encouraged me to try out my conversational French.

I had always loved the Schubert *Lieder* and British folk-songs I had learnt at school. Now through records in music lessons and the stimulation of friends whose knowledge of this esoteric art-form was greater than mine, I was introduced to the classics. I cut my musical teeth on the 'Warsaw Concerto' and Handel's 'Arrival of the Queen of Sheba' and progressed to Bach chorales and fugues.

My aunt, as I've already mentioned, did not care for 'sympathy music'. 'Es rauscht mir im Kop', she would say in Yiddish. (It gives me a headache.)

Her preference was for the waltzes and foxtrots she had stored in her Japanese gramophone cabinet. These had titles like 'Over the Waves' and 'When eyes of blue are fooling you', tunes to which she and my uncle had danced in their youth. There were also tearjerkers like 'My Yiddishe Momma' sung by Sophie Tucker and a rude song with a refrain of 'Oi, yoi yoi oi, tootsie mootsie darling dear' whose exact meaning they refused to tell me. They were pleasant enough, but I was ready for more sophisticated fare. So I remember spending a chilly evening in what was inaptly named the living-room wrapped in my overcoat, in order to listen to Beethoven's Ninth Symphony, while my aunt pottered about the warm kitchen. It was worth it!

The greatest delight of all was the dramatic society. As often happens in a community, there was one ruling spirit in an otherwise unremarkable department who had the energy to give more than was strictly demanded in the course of duty. She occasionally took our class at this stage when our regular teacher was away. Her way of treating her pupils was different from the wary approach (possibly justified by the unpredictable behaviour of adolescents) of some of her colleagues. Miss Sprague actually looked at you with approval and made you feel that your views were of value. However, her most memorable contribution to our lives was her annual production of the school play. I had already had small parts in various little entertainments. In these I was able to exploit my sense of the dramatic and my ability to perform in front of an audience. Perhaps this channelled some of the emotions to which I had blocked access.

At any rate, the excitement of being picked for a major acting part in a production of *Twelfth Night*, learning the lines, the fun of rehearsals, all these made life glow for the many weeks of preparation. After the drabness of the war-years there was the pleasure of trying on colourful costumes – long dresses for the girl characters and doublet and hose for the 'men'. (Being a single-sex school, we had to have girls acting the parts of male characters – Shakespeare's problem in reverse!) We giggled at beards stuck on with spirit-gum and towels used to smooth out unwanted curves in supposed male characters. Then there was the novelty of spreading the sticks of Leichner greasepaint onto our young faces – pale shades for the girls, emphasised by carmine lipstick, and darker shades for the 'men'. When lighting and music were added to this, a transient but beautiful work of art, the sum of many individual efforts, took shape. On the day of the performance, peeping from behind the curtains was strictly forbidden. Tension mounted as we heard the buzz of the audience. The hush and eager anticipation before curtain-up is something those of us who were involved in it will never forget. For the next two hours or so we concentrated on repeating the lines, gestures and 'business' we had so diligently rehearsed. Then all too soon the magic was over, though the memory of it has stayed undimmed.

In other repects our school served us less brilliantly. There was no attempt to present us with literature that in any way reflected our experience. The names we knew in our circle were foreign names – German or Russian or anglicised versions of these. There were Rosenblatts and Yankovitches and Cohens. In our books the names were always Anglo-Saxon. Many of my contemporaries were the daughters of second-generation immigrants, but in the novels that we read the ancestors of the characters had usually come over with the Conqueror. Thus grew up among us a subterranean culture which never surfaced in lessons.

One of my friends discovered a book called *The Education of Hyman Kaplan* which had us howling with laughter. It describes in vivid detail how a bevy of immigrants to New York of varying ethnic origins proceeded to murder the English (or American) language. The leading character in this group was the eponymous Hyman Kaplan, abetted by a Miss Mitnik, a Mr Plonsky and others. In charge of the class was the long-suffering Mr Parkhill (pronounced Pokheel). Their forays into mutual criticism of grammar, spelling and syntax, all of them idiosyncratic, left us in stitches. We could think of numerous examples of similar mispronunciations and misunderstandings. Hadn't my aunt, on being asked by a door-to-door salesman whether she would like to buy an Airwick, replied:

'Ve don't have trouble vit earvigs here'?

Reading this farrago of linguistic-errors, we were encouraged to have a go ourselves. I still remember a piece written by one of us entitled 'De debait fin de hussing', in which several

125

characters discuss housing policy. One of them sums up with the words:

'Vot I say is, let bechelors hev flets, mit spinsters also. Femilis should hev husses.'

In our 'official' essays we wrote decorous pieces on imaginary days in the country and pet animals, our experience of both being minimal! We were taught all the minutiae of grammar from conjunctions to adverbial clauses of time, all the figures of speech from alliteration to zeugma and the poetic metres from spondees to anapests. This fiendish attention to detail enabled me to know the 'rules' of spelling and grammar so well that I was often in later years asked to adjudicate in disputes over these among my colleagues. Though not ungrateful for this knowledge, which certainly has its uses, I could wish that we had been encouraged to explore a little our feelings about the momentous events that were taking place all around us. It was like being given all the techniques for making a dress, but never putting them into an actual garment. Maybe the reason was that these subjects were too loaded for comfort.

Around this time one of our teachers had written a mini-pageant of school-life. One of my classmates and I were asked to do the fifth-form part of it. I had to come on to the stage with a look of doom. Her lines were:

'Hallo, Joan! Why what's the matter?
Surely you've not ceased to chatter!'

My gloomy reply was:

'School Certificate this year
And I'm bound to fail, I fear.'

To which her riposte was:

'Then I'm sorry for the rest!
For you know you're quite the best!'

A piece of tomfoolery, but in reality I was working hard to achieve a good School Certificate. I practised French translation, taking care to pick *le mot juste*; conscientiously revised the *Aeneid* for the Latin exam; tested myself on science-facts. The question now was – what next?

My aunt and uncle had kept me at school for two years beyond the statutory leaving-age of fourteen. My aunt felt it was now time I went out into the world to earn a living. Many of the daughters of her contemporaries had done a secretarial course and got good jobs as shorthand typists. They had meta-morphosed into smart young women with polished nails, high heels and fashionable hair-dos. To my aunt this was a con-siderable achievement. She regarded being a 'sacretary', as she pronounced it, with something like awe. In some ways she was right: it would have done me good to learn a practical skill and have a taste of the reality of the working world to add to my bookish fantasies. However, my gut feeling was in line with Pope's couplet:

> A little learning is a dangerous thing.
> Drink deep or taste not the Pierian spring!

I had tasted the spring and found it too tantalising not to drink deeper. So now began a nagging campaign to be allowed to stay into the Sixth Form, one which had the backing of my teachers. Eventually I was allowed to continue my education after passing in all my eight School Certificate subjects, several of them with distinction.

For some time I had been a sporadic member of a Zionist club that was held at our synagogue. Part of the attraction was the handsome young man from Berlin who ran the club. There were also other girls and boys of my age. Our activities included nothing more daring than folk-dancing and rambles along the towpath of the river Lea, but it was a first step into the grown-up world of dalliance and a pleasant change from the single-sex environment of my school. There was, however, a more serious purpose to the club. It was called 'Bnei Akivah' – the children of Rabbi Akivah. Its motto was 'Torah ve Avodah' – religion and work. Here I learned about the Zionist interpretation of history: for two thousand years the Jewish people had been dispersed in other people's countries where they had been treated as unwelcome guests by intolerant host-communities, the final proof of this being the Nazi extermination camps. The only remedy was to have a country of our own, to reclaim the land which had been ours before the Diaspora. I had had my first inkling of Zionism in Vienna when I saw in some Jewish houses the blue and white boxes with maps of Palestine on them which were used to collect money to buy land. Now I heard about leaders like Theodor Herzl and Chaim Weizmann who had campaigned for the establishment of a Jewish state in Palestine and the Balfour Declaration which had made it possible.

The religious part was far in excess of what I had been brought up to: it entailed interpreting literally the commandment 'Remember the Sabbath day to keep it holy!' This meant not doing anything on that day that could be thought of as work: no sewing, shopping, travelling on buses. As I was no longer prepared to run errands for my aunt on the Sabbath, I had to endure her heavy sarcasm about my sudden fanaticism.

Was I planning to marry a rabbi? she would ask, slyly winking her eyes one moment and shaking her head in mock horror the next. She need not have worried, for when I happened to have a spell away from the other members of the club I found myself riding on buses and doing all the things I used to do on the Sabbath without great feelings of guilt. I recognised then that my conversion to Orthodoxy, though sincere at the time, was a passing fad and gave it up without regret.

My links with Palestine were reinforced by letters (in German) from my aunt and the arrival of intriguing wooden boxes containing raisins, almonds and oranges tasting fresher than the ones we could buy in the shops. There were also letters from my cousin (in English). He had volunteered for the British Army in the desert straight from school and was now demobbed and trying to take up again his interrupted education. I was reading accounts in the newspapers of clashes between the underground movements of the Stern Gang and Haganah and the British Army which was out there under the terms of the Mandate which had put them in charge of the area. I was horrified at the idea of my people fighting British soldiers. I was ignorant of the balance of power the British were trying to keep between Jews and Arabs, but also of the excessive zeal with which they were keeping out starving survivors from the concentration camps. I took these conflicts very personally and used to pour out my dismay to my cousin, pleading for a non-violent solution. His reply was uncompromising: two thousand years of non-violence had fed our people straight into Hitler's gas chambers and the only language politicians understood was armed struggle. I agonised even more when the British, callous in their turn, executed a young Zionist called Dov Grüner. It seemed that the end of the world war had not brought the universal peace we craved.

Meanwhile, having won my own battle to stay on at school, I was now in the Sixth Form. I had originally thought of studying science subjects, but had changed my mind, partly because the Arts subjects came more easily to me, but possibly also because the sciences with their somewhat arid logic lacked the emotional appeal of literature. I therefore chose what seems to me now a narrow spectrum of subjects: English, French, German and Latin. I enjoyed them all with the possible exception of Roman history. What they would lead to I did not know, but I was determined to get to the University, which was the next focus of my efforts.

9 • New horizons

In many ways, life was now opening up for me. While we were evacuated we had not had the use of a car and in any case, no one was then in the mood for major outings, so for me Devon consisted of the triangle bounded by school, the library and the recreation-ground. To these were added a few excursions – to Brixham and Oddicombe Beach with my foster parents and a walk from school to the picturesque village of Cockington and its forge. Now that the war was over, my aunt and I spent a few days amid the palms and boarding-houses of Bournemouth and on some weekends my uncle took us in his taxi on day-trips to Westcliff. His cab was old and liable to break down on long journeys, but we usually made it in the end, with my aunt offering unhelpful advice and my uncle cutting her short with the only unkind word I can remember him using: a succinct 'Sherrrup!' as he peered under the bonnet to locate the problem.

I was hungry for new experiences and welcomed each release from the chains of wartime restrictions. I greatly enjoyed a school-trip to St. Albans to see relics of the Roman town of Verulamium. In the museum everybody gathered round the small glass case containing the excavated remains of a baby whose death, the guide hinted with grisly enjoyment, had not been accidental. Another memorable trip was to Knole in Kent, my first sight of a stately home since my visit to the Hofburg in Vienna. The sheer splendour of the silver hangings in the room where Queen Elizabeth had slept, the armour and rich carvings, made a lasting impression on me. To these visual feasts was added another dimension: a benevolent County Council paid for London schoolchildren to be taken to

130

Sadler's Wells to a performance of *The Magic Flute*. It must have been hastily organised because I remember the conductor singing with the Queen of Night who seemed uncertain of her shrilly menacing aria, but for me, hearing again the Austrian lilt of Mozart's music, there was magic in more than the title of the opera.

Socially, life was beginning again too. During the war most of our energy had been devoted to sheer daily survival and adapting to the changing demands of each phase of the war. Now we were like animals coming out of hibernation, feeling the first timid rays of the sun. In our little family weekends became a time for entertaining. The unlived-in living-room took on warmth and colour as a fire glowed cheerfully in the grate. The large mahogany table was laid with the best china and the middle covered with savoury dishes. There were slices of Dutch herring on a long glass fish-shape and chopped herring on another, flanked by a large platter of various kinds of fried fish and bowls of salad. On a tall stand waited a sample of my aunt's baking: a yeast-cake, well-risen and light of texture which was one of her specialities. My uncle, dressed in dark suit and spotless white shirt, officiated at the sideboard, smiling benignly as he poured drinks for the visitors and for me my favourite yellow advocaat with a blob of red cherry brandy. Some of the guests were relatives of my uncle returned from evacuation, others friends or cousins of my aunt. They were unsophisticated but friendly people.

My own circle was also enlarging. My friend Doris introduced me to her family. Her home was the complete opposite of mine: my aunt spent a good deal of time on cleaning and polishing every item of furniture and household equipment so that you could see your reflection in it. Meals were promptly served and promptly cleared away. Clothes were carefully washed and ironed and stored in appropriate places. Not so in my friend's home where disorder was rampant in the kitchen and routine unknown. Her mother's explanation for this state of affairs was: 'It was such a lovely day, I left all the housework.' This seemed a sensible idea till one noticed that not-so-lovely days had a similar outcome.

What made my friend's home so attractive despite its disorder were the very things which were lacking in mine: music and books and lively conversation. Doris's mother was a small but formidable woman with a mordant wit who was much given to expatiating on *The Forsyte Saga*. She had been the pianist who accompanied the silent films in the cinema owned by her father and often sat down to tinkle on the ancient piano in her front room tunes from the shows of her youth. Sometimes her husband would prop his violin under his chin to give a rendering of the Cavetina by Raff or play 'Nights of Gladness' in a hyped-up version of palm court style. Doris's father, although he earned his living as a craftsman in the fur-trade, had had a grammar-school education. He and his offspring had a flair for punning and a way of twisting language. After the literal-mindedness of my aunt and uncle I found this very amusing. If he thought someone was tedious, he would say 'He's a bit gillow' (Waring and Gillow). Or he would refer to bread as 'daylight' (broad daylight) and use other extensions of ordinary speech which made me chuckle appreciatively.

Doris's younger brother was at this time a street urchin much under the thumb of his sister who ordered him about unmercifully:

'Wash your hands! Take off those muddy boots! Don't come in here!'

He seemed unperturbed by this treatment, but it made me wonder for the first time what it would be like to have a younger brother. I felt he was rather wasted on Doris.

Doris's elder brother, by contrast, was a medical student and regarded with some awe. The first time I met him he was half perching on the edge of a table. I saw a young man with woolly dark hair, very pointed ears like a pixie's and deep-set blue eyes with a mocking twinkle. His feet, which dangled off the floor, were clad in plimsolls and I noticed they were rather small for a man. All in all, he was what the French call *beau laid* – attractive in a rugged sort of way. I don't know whether my academic reputation had preceded me, but he challenged me immediately with the question:

'Do you think the family is the basic unit of society?'

I did my best to respond from my limited experience. It was exhilarating to bandy words with him, but as he left the room to continue his studies, I had the feeling that for once I had come off worst in the exchange.

* * *

The end of a year in the Sixth Form brought the exciting prospect of another treat: my first journey abroad since that fateful crossing of the North Sea so unwillingly undertaken. The proposed trip was a school-journey to Switzerland. There was one practical problem for me: all the other girls, being British-born, could be entered on a communal passport. This would not be possible for me.

'It would make things easier if you were to become naturalised', explained the teacher in charge of the party. I knew my foster parents were naturalised British citizens, so this seemed an apt solution. After filling in a form, I received a summons to an interview at the Home Office. I was shown to a chair facing a desk behind which stood an official. He handed me a declaration to sign. I did so and he asked me what I thought naturalisation entailed. The answer was obvious to me, so I replied: 'Loyalty to your adopted country.'

This seemed to satisfy him and he shook my hand before I left. I could now be included in the school passport.

My German passport with the word 'stateless' stamped on its first page was buried deep in some half-forgotten drawer. We would be staying in the German-speaking part of Switzerland. Of the fact that this experience would somehow connect with the Continent I had left eight years ago I was only dimly conscious as for the time being, all other thoughts were swept aside by the excitement of the preparations. My case was packed with a few necessities and as I left, my aunt thrust a bag of sandwiches into my hand with the words: 'And whatever you do, don't climb an Alp!'

I remember little of the crossing, but I have vivid memories of the Belgian train that stood ready for us at the quayside. We were travelling fourth class, which meant long hours of squirming on slatted wooden seats. The floor of our compartment had not seen a scrubbing-brush for many years, so when during some horseplay one of our party 'accidentally' hit the ground, her blue and white striped uniform blouse was crisscrossed with black bars of soot. The train skirted the Belgian border and took us past depressingly grey and run-down townships in the industrial districts of Alsace and Lorraine. Its pace was slow and the journey long, so we dozed off. Waking up in the early morning light, we were rewarded by a sight of the Alps. I had never seen mountains before and there they were – high, craggy and topped with snow – just like in the picture-books!

More than a day after we had set out from England, we arrived at Einsiedeln, near Zurich, and were driven to our hotel. Despite our tiredness, there were squeals of delight when we were shown to our rooms, each with a wooden ceiling and clothes-cupboard, two beds covered by a brightly coloured counterpane, and a spotless washbasin. Our evening-meal was generous and for me reminiscent of childhood: *Wiener Schnitzel* and lettuce dressed with vinegar. The spring water that was served with it, ice-cold and purer than any I had ever tasted, was instantly refreshing.

Next day, we explored the village, exclaimed at the tinkle of bells coming from the cows on a nearby pasture, and wandered round the shops in search of such presents and souvenirs as our small amount of pocket-money would stretch to. We noticed the shop-signs, many bearing names ending in 'li', and I tried to understand the Schweizerdeutsch, a sister-dialect of the High German I was more used to. Later, we swam or paddled in a nearby river where our wet legs and exposed necks made ready targets for a swarm of vicious biting flies.

The following day, we set off on a longish ramble in preparation for a bigger challenge: contrary to my aunt's advice, we were going to climb an Alp! Behind our guest-house loomed the shapes of two mountains – one reaching up to the sky and almost conical, the other, lower and more squat. They were known as the Grosse and Kleine Mythen. Our aim, or so our teachers declared, was to climb the higher of the two. Our faces blenched a little at this news and some of the girls, believing that discretion was the better part of valour, dropped out at once.

Of the people who decided to make the assent, most were members of school teams already well-known for their athletic prowess. I was not among these, for although I enjoyed vaulting over horses and climbing ropes in the gym, my co-ordination in ball-games was uncertain and erratic. Sometimes I would achieve a remarkable catch which made the team-captain look at me with new eyes, but at other times I would myself be caught day-dreaming in deep field, letting the ball trickle undisturbed past me, to the rage of the keener spirits. There was some surprise, therefore, when I expressed the intention of joining the Mythen party.

The mountain, although it seemed to be near our guest-house, was in fact several miles away. We trudged towards it expectantly. When we reached it, it seemed impossibly tall, but not difficult to climb. A path wound round it like a spiral spring. We negotiated the first few coils singing cheerfully. Then, as the heat of the sun grew more powerful and the distance to the top diminished only slowly, we saved our breath. Half-way up, some of the girls decided they had had enough and began the descent. About ten of us, including one of the teachers, opted for pressing on to the top. Carrying on now became a matter of sheer willpower as we toiled round and round and up and up. Near the end of the climb, my heart was pounding fiercely and my lungs were ready to burst. Only an obstinate determination kept me on that path.

'Just a little further!' I kept saying to myself. I can still remember the sheer triumph of standing on the top, looking in lordly fashion down on the valley 6,000 feet below. No gift of money could have equalled that sense of achievement. We drew many deep breaths of the pure mountain air, rested, swallowed our drinks greedily and prepared for the descent. This too had its problems, as one's spine was jolted by the perpetual downward movement and I had to learn to splay my feet to steady myself. The level walk back to the hotel seemed as nothing by comparison.

The villagers of Einsiedeln had gone out of their way to welcome us. Whether this had something to do with their admiration for British resistance to the German threat during the war I don't know, but we were told that they were going to give us a concert before we left. This consisted of a special performance by the Yodel Choir dressed in the broad leather braces and baggy trousers of their national costume. Their voices, honed to a fine resonance, hallooed and reverberated to the rafters of the village hall. We in turn entertained them by singing some English songs and miming the movements of an imaginary orchestra to a record of the 'Wilhelm Tell' Overture. The teacher in charge of our party had asked me to make a speech of thanks in German. I spent some time preparing this and felt a great sense of pride and responsibility when I stepped onto the platform to thank our hosts in something like their own language. Next day there were sad farewells, but as we climbed into our railway-compartment, who should be there to meet us but the Yodel Choir in full strength, serenading us out of the station?

Coming back from the clean mountain-villages of Switzerland to grimy, war-damaged London was something of an anti-climax. For me, the trip back to Europe had been a tantalising experience. It was like peeping between slightly spread fingers at something one is not supposed to see. I had not dared to look too closely or think too deeply. When something reminded me forcibly of my former existence, down came the shutters. I had at the time no information about the fate of the relatives I had left behind. Of my parents' extended families I knew a few names from remarks dropped in conversation, but where they had lived and what sort of people they were, I had hardly any idea. I felt their loss only as a generalised ache which I did my best to smother with more immediate concerns. I was abetted in this by well-meaning comforters like my aunt who would say, if any suspicion of a sensitive subject like my orphaned state came up: 'You've got your whole life before you.'

There was truth of a kind in this.

My attitude to things German had the same air of vague unreality. This was brought out by an essay competition at my school. There was to be a prize for the best essay in French on a topic chosen by a former French teacher. We were all encouraged to enter for this. The subject for that year was 'Should the German people be banished from the community of civilised nations?' or words to that effect. My answer to this question was an emphatic: 'No, for hasn't Germany produced a Beethoven as well as a Hitler?' ('l'Allemagne n'a-t-elle pas produit un Beethoven aussi bien qu'un Hitler?') Needless to say, I won the prize.

* * *

The war had ended in a surge of optimism: never again was the human race to be plagued by such aggression, and the United Nations Organisation was formed to make sure of this. As teenagers we believed that it was possible to create a better world, for who would want to go through the suffering of the last ten years again? My ideas were being formed by the BBC and other sources. My uncle, a Labour Party supporter, bought the *Daily Herald* from time to time. Its demand for a welfare state along the lines advocated by the Beveridge Report seemed to make sense.

'Security from the cradle to the grave' was a slogan with wide appeal. Poverty was to be banished. There was to be a National Health Service. Free false teeth, free glasses were soon to be available to all, and obese ladies of my aunt's generation discovered that they suffered from 'severe visceroptosis', which enabled them to buy a corset of alarming rigidity at reduced cost. The 'Spirella lady' with her dictum of 'you need a good support' was much in demand, and accidental contact with one of her clients felt like an encounter with an armadillo.

One of my friends was politically more extreme than the rest of us. She would play the Internationale on her gramophone, praise the Russian Revolution and go out leafletting for the Communist Party. A few of their ideas seemed attractive and we had long discussions about these, but despite my vast ignorance of political detail and recent history, I felt there was something not quite right about the system.

'If you have only one party, what happens if you don't like the way they're running the country? You can't get rid of them.'

Her reply was: 'But the party are carrying out the will of the people, so there's no need to get rid of them.'

I was not convinced.

Another source of new ideas was Doris. She had got hold of a copy of Shaw's *Intelligent Woman's Guide to Capitalism and Socialism*. I don't remember much of the detail of the book except that I enjoyed the Shavian wit, but one idea leapt at me off the pages: Shaw said that you're not obliged to like your relatives. To me this was a liberating thought. I had been wrestling for some time with guilt about the resentment I felt towards my aunt for some of her narrow-mindedness. It now seemed that my feelings were not as wicked as I had imagined.

By now I was in the Upper Sixth Form. This entailed, besides the honour and glory of being a prefect and House Captain, a seemingly endless succession of examinations. I found I had a quick mind and a good memory. Both of these served me well in timed tests. My teachers, keen to exploit these assets, no doubt for good reasons, put me in for a variety of scholarship and university entrance examinations. One of these was the Intercollegiate examination which provided successful candidates with exhibitions and scholarships to various London University colleges. I was entered as a student of Modern Languages and duly did my translations and essays in French and German. Some weeks later, I received a letter asking me to come for an interview to Westfield College.

When I arrived, there were students in academic gowns to greet me and show me round the unimpressive but friendly brick building. Eventually I was ushered into the presence of the Principal, Mary Stocks. She had an angular face and sharp eyes which fixed me with a piercing gaze. She began by asking me about my favourite books and hobbies. She then startled me by saying: 'I see from your application-form that you are Jewish. Does that mean that if you came here we would need to have special pots and pans for you?'

Stung by this, I replied at once: 'No. I believe in the ethical basis of the Jewish religion, but I don't regard the dietary laws as relevant today.'

There was a 'humph' of approval from the Principal, and some days later, I received a letter, offering me an Exhibition at Westfield College. I could begin my studies there in the autumn of 1948 if I accepted it.

Meanwhile there came another summons to an interview, this time at Queen Mary College. On this occasion I was faced by a whole Academic Board. The question I remember being asked was: 'Why do you want to study Modern Languages?' My reply was: 'Well, actually, I would really like to read for a degree in English.' The feeling that I no longer wanted to study Modern Languages must have been growing inside me for some time. I find it hard to explain why. Perhaps part of me felt that I wanted to get access to literature without the intervention of translations and dictionaries. I probably also felt unconsciously that a degree in French and German would have entailed staying in those countries. The one clear instinct I had, despite my blurred perceptions of what had happened in Europe, was that it would be impossible for me to set foot on German soil. It may also have had something to do with my growing suppression of my Austrian past.

After the members of the Board had recovered from their surprise at this about-turn, the gentleman who had been questioning me, probably the Head of the Modern Languages Faculty, gave way to the Professor of English. In his strong Scottish accent he asked:

'And why, Miss Immerdauer, do you want to read for a degree in English?'

My answer,

'Because English has one of the most interesting literatures', seemed to please him, and some days later, I received a letter, offering me a scholarship to Queen Mary College. I found it hard to make up my mind which college to choose and did not know whom to turn to for advice. My eventual choice was arbitrary: I had spent seven years in an all-female environment at school. I felt it was now time to meet the other half of the human race, and so I chose Queen Mary College.

* * *

I was distracted from these considerations by a pleasant surprise. My mother had some distant relatives who had managed to escape to England just before the war. They were two sisters, one of whom had a daughter of about my age. Apparently my mother had asked them to visit me in London, and this they did soon after my arrival. I imagine that they reported back that I was in reasonably good shape. It was not until quite recently that I realised that Eva, one of the sisters, had actually seen my mother after I had left. She did not make this clear until just before she died, a few years ago. I wish now I had been able to question her about my mother's situation at the time.

Soon after this visit, the war broke out, we were all evacuated and lost contact with each other. Now, in 1948, out of the blue there came a letter addressed to me with a Cornish postmark. It turned out that Eva's daughter, who had also sat for the Intercollegiate Scholarship, had received a list of the successful candidates, on which she recognised my name. The letter contained an invitation to spend two weeks with her family in Cornwall. I was thrilled at this prospect.

I was now about to leave the safe haven of the school I had attended for nearly five years. It had taught me some sharp lessons about rivalry and the fickleness of schoolgirl friendships, but had also nourished my developing intellect in many ways. Earlier on, leaving would have been a daunting experience, but now I sang 'Lord, dismiss us with thy blessing', the leaving hymn which was guaranteed to bring a lump to the throat, with equanimity, buoyed up by the thought that there were more exciting times ahead. I had finished my examinations and come out with the offer of two Open Scholarships. I had been House Captain and Deputy Head Girl. Now I could look forward to taking up my place at the University.

A week later, finding myself alone in a compartment on the last lap of the long train journey to Redruth, I sang all the songs I knew in German and English. I was welcomed at the station by Eva, her husband, and daughter Helen. They told me that Eva and her daughter had been evacuated to Devon during the war. They had moved to this small market town when Eva's husband was offered a job there after being demobbed from the army. Their home, part of a converted hotel, had a strange layout and was equipped with the severe furniture known as 'utility' which was being produced at the time. I was struck by the contrast between this and my aunt's massively ornate mahogany pieces.

It was a joy to meet people from my home town who did their best to make my stay a happy one. Eva was a woman in early middle age with finely moulded features and greying wavy hair pulled back from her face. Her husband was a quiet man with a quizzical expression, and her daughter, a plumply attractive teenager. There was also much to explore in the surrounding countryside. Cornwall was a fascinating county with its granite houses, relics of tin-mines, and everywhere – the sea. Names which had been only storybook titles for me until then took on reality. We visited Frenchman's Creek and St. Ives, perched on a steep hill with cliffs dropping down to the shore. White cottages with vivid doors nestled among its slopes, gulls uttered their piercing cries and the cold, electric blue waters of the Atlantic lapped against the beach.

As it was Helen's birthday, there was a party for her schoolfriends. We chatted and giggled and played Blind Man's Buff and Musical Chairs as though we hadn't a care in the world. Yesterday was obliterated. I don't remember anyone in the course of that holiday saying a word about my parents' fate or that of the parents my hosts had left behind in Vienna. What had happened in Europe was not referred to and I was unable to open the subject myself. That these people held the key to some knowledge I badly needed I could not allow myself to realise at the time.

* * *

My return to London brought more good news: I had done well in my Higher School Certificate and gained a distinction in English Literature, thus justifying my choice of a degree subject. A State Scholarship was added to my other awards. This, although the grant was a modest one, would give me the wherewithal to pursue my studies. My uncle and aunt had long been resigned to the fact that I was determined to follow my own bent. I think they felt a secret pride in my academic success, tempered with some anxiety about the unpredictable market-value of an Arts degree.

I had achieved so much against all the odds. I can now see how this was built on the consistency of my foster parents' care for me. They had spared no effort to look after my physical needs and much else besides. It would have been asking more than was reasonable of such simple human beings that they should be able to eliminate totally the effects of the quite extraordinary trauma I had suffered. True, Jewish people were inured to hostility and small-scale aggression such as the pogroms that had brought thousands of them to Britain and the United States, but genocide was something else. Not surprisingly, neither they nor I were able to come to terms with such a horror.

It would have been difficult for people who did not know me to place me at this stage. I had shed my foreign accent, and my straight hair and regular features did not proclaim a Semitic parentage. In my mind I had half-yielded to my teachers' well-meant suggestion that I was an ordinary English girl, without realising the chasm that separated my experiences from those of my classmates brought up in conventional English families. On the other hand, I had no contact with survivors from concentration camps or detailed knowledge of the deportations and massacres that had occurred in Europe. If such knowledge was available at this time, I avoided it. My adolescent shoulders were simply not strong enough to bear the burden of such a vast atrocity which, as I later discovered, had destroyed dozens of members of my parents' large extended families. This meant that my hold on reality was brittle and my identity blurred. I managed to survive by concentrating on the present and shutting out painful topics, but they had a way of intruding disturbingly in unguarded moments. The 'I' who entered Queen Mary College was the sum of many horrific experiences and confusing sets of values, as well as the recipient of much that was kind, positive and enlightening. Still, I was young and could not be gloomy for too long, so I determined to enjoy the opportunities offered by the next phase of my life.

Queen Mary College opened many doors for me, both social and intellectual. Freed from the constraints of the school timetable, I threw myself into a variety of activities. I listened to, and occasionally participated in, union debates, and attended extra-curricular lectures on philosophy, music, architecture and other subjects. I went to a local exhibition of Van Gogh paintings which introduced me to the visual arts. I had once gone to the National Gallery, but found the range of styles there bewildering. Here was a small corner I could explore with enjoyment and I revelled in the bold colours and emphatic shapes of the objects in the pictures.

By way of social life, there were lunchtime and Saturday night hops. At these you might be lucky enough to be asked to dance with one of the college's heart-throbs, usually a student newly demobbed from the Forces whose poise derived from his greater maturity. Alternatively, you might be stuck with a pimply youth who trod on your toes and smiled sheepishly in apology. In addition to the informal dances, the colleges held annual balls which were grander affairs. Eva's daughter Helen had gained a place at King's College and a friend of hers invited me to their student ball. With money earned by working at a tax-office in part of the long vacation, I had bought an evening-gown of cerise taffeta. It felt very romantic to dance the evening away in such finery. It was the done thing to end such an evening with a parting kiss, but one didn't lightly go further, for the code of the time forbade the easy sexual opportunism of more recent years.

Queen Mary College boasted a grand pillared entrance, a spacious circular library modelled on the Bodleian at Oxford and a tiered lecture-theatre, the Hatton. Other parts of the building ranged from the unprepossessing to the positively dingy. The latter included a basement canteen known as 'The Bunhole'. Here, undeterred by the lingering smell of baked beans, the steam from boiled puddings and the green drain-pipes which were the only prominent feature of the room, we spent many hours discussing literature and the problems of the world. For the first time I met people from Yorkshire, the Midlands and Wales. The acquaintance was superficial, as our focus was on our course rather than on their backgrounds, but I like to think they broadened my outlook a little.

The society that attracted me most was the dramatic society. This seemed a natural progression from the roles I had under-taken at school. Rehearsals were fun as we chatted and laughed and linked arms to practise the Palais Glide while waiting for our turn to go on stage. The first production was Ben Jonson's comedy *The Silent Woman*, a hilarious play about a man who cannot stand noise marrying an apparently dumb woman who turns out to be neither dumb nor a woman. Of all the societies, the dramatic society was the most demanding of time and I well remember our professor's tart comment: 'Many a guid ferrst has gone dune the drramsoc drrain!' There was some truth in this, as I discovered to my cost three years later.

One aspect of the course I didn't relish was Anglo-Saxon literature. This was easier for me to come to grips with than for most of the other students because of my knowledge of

German, yet I found it distasteful because of its glorification of beer and battle. I had little enthusiasm for either. The lecturer who taught us was a Dr Timmer, a charming Dutchman whom we all took a shine to. He called me 'the immortal lady' (my name meant 'everlasting'). He told us he had spent the war years in Holland and that he had once purposely misdirected a German armoured detachment. I warmed to him for that piece of sabotage and wish I had been able to find out more. However, my liking for the man did not increase my enjoyment of his subject.

In addition to a good deal of superficial socialising, I made a few close friends. One of these was Jessica who came from Berlin. She was the first person I got to know well who was a refugee like myself, so that there was some unspoken under-standing between us. Our situations in other ways were com-pletely different: she came from a wealthy family and both her mother and sister had managed to get out of Germany in time. Not only that, but to my amazement, they had actually brought some of their furniture with them so that art nouveau chests and tables filled up the cavernous spaces of their Belsize Park flat. Jessica's mother was perpetually on the telephone to her expatriate cronies and my most enduring image of her is of a woman doing the ironing while cradling the handset on her shoulder as she chatted away volubly in German.

One element in my course of studies I found hard to come to terms with: the Christian. Most of the novels and poems I had read so far had little specific religious content. The novels con-centrated on the interplay of character, and the Romantic poets whose work we studied in the sixth form only worshipped Nature. Now I was confronted with the sermons of Donne. 'Ask not for whom the bell tolls' and 'No man is an island' made an immediate appeal to me, but what was I to make of conjectures about the Second Coming? Worse still of Herbert, given to musing about church floors and windows. I noticed the tenderness that crept into our lecturer's voice as he quoted some well-known devotional lines which left me feeling puzzled and alienated, guilty to be listening to them at all.

145

Most of my fellow-students professed a cheerful agnosticism like my own, so I tried to minimise the effect of this contact with Christian dogma by playing down its importance.

Nevertheless, my developing aesthetic interest prompted me to explore the insides of churches and cathedrals whenever I had the opportunity. I found the buildings fascinating and quite unlike the austere interiors of synagogues, in which images are forbidden and decoration is sparse. From guide-books I puzzled out the difference between Norman and Early and Late Gothic, and learned the vocabulary of nave, chancel, choir-stalls, etc. I savoured the colours of the stained glass windows, though my ignorance of the New Testament prevented me from understanding fully the stories they depicted. The cool, grey stillness, broken at times by the resonant strains of the organ, the aisles with their banners and statuary, the chapels with their quiet invitations to prayer, the beauty and peace that pervaded these buildings – all had for me a compelling attraction. So here was yet another paradox to add to my growing list of contradictions.

10 · *The past revisited*

Three years after I entered Queen Mary College, I graduated, and applied to do teacher-training at the Institute of Education. As for the young man with the woolly hair and deep-set eyes, it was a case of 'Reader, I married him'.

By then he had qualified as a doctor, done some house-jobs in hospital and had a spell in the army in Malaysia. We had corresponded sporadically while he was abroad and I at college, and when he returned to England, smelling of sandal-wood and redolent of the mysteries of the East, I accepted his proposal. I was very young and had not even started my teacher-training course, but I felt constricted by living with my foster parents at this stage of my life and found my aunt's well-intentioned interference in my affairs irritating. There was no possibility of getting into a university hall of residence, as I had a base in London, and living in sin, as it was called in those days, would have given my aunt a heart-attack. We were in love and intended to marry anyway, so why not now?

Marriage for me meant a re-routing of my life. While I did my teacher-training and a year's stint of teaching at an Evening Institute, my husband worked as an assistant in a medical practice. He was then offered a partnership in the practice on condition that I was prepared to help out. I had parted company with science at School Certificate, and knew nothing about medicine, but the new role seemed a welcome break from the serious academic studies of previous years. More importantly, such offers to newly qualified and impecunious doctors were not easy to come by, and we wanted to start a family within the next few years, so I agreed to the metamorphosis and gave up the idea of teaching for a time.

147

The senior partner's wife, a formidable lady, introduced me to my new duties which turned out to be a bizarre mixture: I was to move into the flat vacated by the senior partner which had the surgery premises (a low brick building) at the bottom of the garden. I was to see that the brass plates at both the flat and surgery-ends were kept polished, the surgery cleaned, the drain outside it kept clear of autumn leaves to avoid flooding, and the telephone manned constantly. I was also to act as receptionist and chaperone to my husband during most of the surgeries.

On the day the deal was clinched, we invited my husband's future partner to dinner. I decided to serve Dover sole as a main dish. I remember pushing the fish under the grill with a distinct feeling of helplessness. Translating Beowulf I could have managed with ease, but this, I felt, was outside my sphere of competence. The size of the flame and the amount of time needed for cooking were complete mysteries to me. The result was four objects charred at the edges and dry in the middle. I cut off the burnt bits and gave the guests the better pieces, at which they politely chipped away without comment. Surprisingly, the offer of the practice partnership was not withdrawn.

The years that followed were the busiest of my life. My energies were devoted to answering the ever-shrilling telephone, making good the glaring deficiencies in my domestic skills and bringing up my children – two sons born in 1954 and 1957. There was little time for anything else, though I did keep up my interest in reading and the theatre as best I could. I was living near enough to my foster parents to see them frequently, though my uncle had died suddenly following an operation not long after I was married. My aunt, who survived him by ten years, was deeply upset by this loss. However, she did enjoy being with my children and came regularly to see me with supplies of home-baked biscuits and other offerings. We kept up a thorny but affectionate relationship until she too died suddenly while staying with friends.

Since by this time most of my college-friends had scattered

to the four winds, I found myself needing to make new ones. This made me aware of a problem: the young women I met at my children's nursery school all had mothers, fathers, sisters or brothers and birthplaces they could talk about without strain. I had none of these, so people either made false assumptions about me or perhaps thought me rather close – if they bothered to think about me at all. I felt profoundly ill-at-ease about revealing my true identity, mainly because the subject had become taboo with me, but also probably because of unconscious fears of what prejudices I might arouse if I were too open. Hitherto, my friends in London had been people I had known a long time – even at college there was one student who had been at school with me – which did away with the need for long explanations. Now, being a closet refugee made me an uncomfortable guest to strangers. My husband's family knew all about my story, but there seemed to be some tacit agreement not to talk about it. Even my children, who had been told something of it, when choosing a birthday present for me of a set of continental decorative plates said to my husband: 'We'd better ask if they're Austrian. We don't want to upset Mummy.' They were from Czechoslovakia.

* * *

By chance, one of my acquaintances mentioned that she had read a book called *The Diary of Anne Frank*. As many readers now know, this was a journal kept by a young girl who had lived with her parents, sister and some friends in a secret hiding-place in Amsterdam while Holland was under Nazi occupation. The family had finally been betrayed and taken away to concentration camps where all but the father had died. It was not till many years later that I plucked up enough courage to read the book. I found, unexpectedly, that despite its horrific end, the life of the Frank family as seen through the eyes of the teenage daughter was far from gloomy. Her comments on the interaction of people living at such close quarters were perceptive and, at times, highly amusing. Despite the abnormal circumstances of their existence, she struck me as a very normal, intelligent adolescent, idealistic and intolerant in equal measure.

Although I put off reading the diary, I could not avoid learning about some of the details of Nazi atrocities through the trial of Dr Dering. He had started a libel action against Leon Uris who alleged in a book that the doctor had collaborated with the infamous Dr Mengele in carrying out surgical experiments on Jewish women. A great deal of other information such as of the mass shootings which preceded the construction of the death factories at Auschwitz, Treblinka and other places, came out through witnesses at the trial and was published in the newspapers. I recognised the germ of these horrors from my memories of my last year in Austria, but this was everything I had heard about and feared enlarged to the nth degree.

Harrowing though this knowledge was, it seemed possible to draw a line under those years. After all, this was England and hadn't we fought a war to defeat the scourge of Nazism? It was something of a shock, then, when, only ten years after the end of that war, I noticed that a crowd had gathered near where I lived at Highbury Corner in London and that the speaker was mouthing propaganda that could well have found a place in the Nazi broadsheets of the 1930s. I could not believe my ears. Finding a man with a dog-collar in the audience, I buttonholed him.

'Is this what we fought a war for?' I demanded. 'Why don't you do something about it?'

He made some reply about free speech and that these members of the National Front were a tiny minority who did not represent the real feelings of the British people. I was shaken by this experience and not greatly reassured by the clergyman's words, however rational. I thought of the fate of my young cousins and feared for the safety of my children.

In fact, I had never encountered personal animosity towards me as a Jewess in England, nor had I in my early schooldays read any literature which I recognised as anti-Semitic. *Oliver Twist* I only knew from extracts and was not properly aware that the unpleasant Fagin was a Jew. I did know that the villain of *The Merchant of Venice* was a Jew, but whether by design or accident, the play had never been used for detailed study in any class I was in. I had learned Portia's speech about the 'quality of mercy' as a party-piece without noticing that it was aimed at the supposedly merciless Shylock. It was therefore with a stab of pain that I read one of the essays by Charles Lamb which were set for School Certificate. It was entitled 'Imperfect Sympathies'. Apparently this gentle man, who was so tender to his sister and wrote so feelingly about the children he wished he had, could spare no compassion for Jews. The essay in question was one I had read myself, but not one that had been selected for class-study, so I was left with a nagging feeling of injustice about it. Again, there was nobody I could discuss it with even if I had been able to express what I felt.

Later I came across other writers who made snide anti-Semitic remarks and a story in the *Canterbury Tales* which turned out to be about some wicked Jews who had killed a Christian child, probably to use its blood for the Passover – the blood-libel I dimly remembered hearing about in my child-hood. This story, 'The Prioress's Tale', was regarded by the critics as the highwater mark of mediaeval literature. Despite my admiration for Chaucer, I could not share their opinion, and solved the problem by turning to other authors whose writings were free of this taint.

During my period as a housewife, I had time to think about all this. Though no great Biblical scholar myself, I decided that religion was the cause of all the world's troubles and that I must take on the Establishment single-handed. My first brush was with another local vicar. The parents at the infants' school one of my sons went to were invited to a Harvest Home. I came to it, expecting it to be a clone of the ritual we used to have at my school: displays of loaves and marrows and a spirited rendering of 'We plough the fields and scatter'.

Instead, the vicar asked the children to repeat after him several times a passage from the New Testament. I challenged him about this after the service.

'I don't call that a Harvest Festival. I call that indoctrination.

And why, when you knew you had a group of children of different religions and none at all, did you make no mention of this in your sermon?'

His reply, 'I was giving the children their tradition', had more truth in it than I could acknowledge at the time, but would have been more appropriate in a purely Christian community. Some days later, he sent me a letter stating that he had never felt a trace of anti-Semitism until he met me. I took that as a compliment.

Realising that perhaps I had been a little ambitious in thinking that, like St. Joan, I could work miracles, I joined the Council of Christians and Jews. I thought that in this way I might be able to help to correct the false ideas that Christians and Jews have about each other which lead to mutual intolerance. I could be wrong, or maybe too impatient for swift action, but at the time I found no great enthusiasm for my views in that organisation. In any case, my children were now both at school. I had delayed going back to work through fear of what would happen if I abandoned them too early as my mother had been forced to abandon me. However, I decided it was now time to make a start. Perhaps I could exert more influence, on however small a scale, as a teacher. Therefore I spent the next 25 years – 23 of them at Skinners' School – discussing race-relations, as part of the English curriculum, with groups of pupils of English, Greek, Turkish, Asian and Afro-Caribbean origin. I also helped the school to draw up its anti-racist policy.

In the busy years when I was bringing up my children, I had managed on the surface to keep clear of painful topics, yet they kept coming back to haunt me in moments of solitude. Half-formulated questions whirred about in my brain:

How had my parents died and where?
What horrors did they have to face before then?
What was a day in a concentration camp like?
What did they sleep on if sleep was possible?
What were their last words?
Did they think of me?

Could they recall happier times in their lives?
I had a fantasy of a brutal SS-man noticing my father's name –
Immerdauer – and shouting 'We'll see about that!' as he put
the jackboot in.

How was it possible, I wondered, that a civilised state like
Germany could make murder its official policy?

I sought general answers to these questions through a
course of post-graduate study which included psychology. I
read the work done in the United States by Allport, Adorno
and others. They taught me how prejudices are formed in
people's minds and about the authoritarian personality which
makes itself the measure of all things and rejects anything alien
to it. I learned about stereotyping, the mechanism by which we
lump together all the people of a certain group, and projection,
in which we attribute to them the qualities we despise in ourselves. For instance:

'All Scotsmen are mean.'

'All Americans are vulgar.'

'All Jews are greedy.'

This still could not fully explain what had happened in
Europe.

As for the other questions, slowly I braced myself to read the
literature of the concentration camps and find out how it had
been done. First all Jews were herded into ghettos to make it
easier to round them up. This was followed by deportation to
the death camps where SS-men selected the small minority
who were kept alive a little longer to work, and consigned the
young, the old and the sick to be gassed immediately. I owe a
great debt to Primo Levi, Kitty Hart and others who had the
courage to write about events so painful that it took them years
to be able to communicate their experiences. Also from Martin
Gilbert's *The Holocaust – A Jewish Tragedy* I gained knowledge
of the whole pattern of mass destruction in every country the
Germans occupied. There was no joy in such reading, but I
found it was a relief to know the facts, as my own fantasies had
an even greater power to disturb me than the reality itself.

Other gaps I now discovered in my life were concerned with

153

my own identity. I knew so little about my parents and their families, apart from a few scraps of information, and felt I had to know more. The only person who might be able to tell me anything was my father's youngest sister in Israel. In 1970 I decided to take a trip, my second by air, to see her.

My aunt, recently widowed, had moved to a small flat near the main shopping-street and not far from the seashore in Tel Aviv. On her kitchen wall I noticed a framed piece of embroidery in the cross-stitch I remembered on some of my mother's needlework. My aunt's features bore a close resemblance to my father's: the same prominent nose, deep-set blue eyes and dark hair now streaked with grey. As we sat on her balcony among her potted palms and shaded by an awning against the fierce sun, I tried to talk to her. It was not easy because the only language we had in common was my halting German and the subject I most wanted to talk about opened many wounds.

She brought out pictures of several members of our family. One was of three of her sisters, beautiful women with the upswept hairstyles and high necklines of Edwardian times. Another came to me as a thunderbolt: it was of my grandmother seated, and standing behind her, my father in the uniform of an Austrian Army officer in the First World War.

This killed one of my illusions at a stroke. Seeing my father led away by the SS without a struggle, I had assumed that he would have avoided military service. This was clearly not so. Though not war-like by nature, he had not shirked his duty when called up. The Austrian Army at the time was not rich in literate men among its conscripts, and as my father could read and write and speak several languages, he was ordered to serve as an interpreter. This was to count for nothing with the SS.

Another of my illusions was that my family were all desperately poor. There was a grain of truth in this belief. Contrary to popular opinion, a large section of the Jewish community in Poland did live in dire poverty, as seen in the poignant photographs of Vishniac. But not all. My grandmother, it seems, had a hard time bringing up eight children (one of them – my aunt Irene – was a posthumous child) after her husband's untimely death. My grandfather, Israel Immerdauer, a sombrely dressed and bearded man according to his photographs, had been the Talmudic scholar of the family and had not left his widow well provided for. His brother, Laser, however, whom I had heard my father mention because of his large number of children – fourteen, I believe – was a successful businessman who had obtained an appointment from the Austrian Emperor for the sale of tobacco in Lvov. He figures in George Clare's book *Last Waltz in Vienna*. By the 1930s my grandmother was a very old lady and only three of her daughters were left in Poland. These were fairly prosperous and when my uncle Sigmund, Irene's husband, suggested to them that there were bad times ahead for Jews in that country and invited them and their families to join him in Palestine, the reponse was:

'We're doing well here. What is there in Palestine? Sand and Arabs?'

My aunt and uncle had indeed had to put up with many hardships when they emigrated. At first, there were no refrigerators, proper pavements or schools for their son, yet they managed in time to build up a successful shoe-store. The others, sadly, paid a high price for their misjudgement.

I was eager for the kind of information that people with an uninterrupted upbringing take for granted: I wanted to know what sort of person my father was, what he was like as a boy, and grasped avidly at any straw. Aunt Irene told me about the time she and my father (they were close in age) had played in the nearby woods as children and that, after she had lost her shoes in a stream, they had put off going home for fear of my grandmother's wrath. She also told me of my grandmother's wish that my father should go to a rabbinical college, but that he had chosen to go to a commercial college instead. I was intrigued to hear that he had spent part of his first wages as a junior clerk in going to the theatre, an interest I could have shared with him. She also remembered the whole family going to the synagogue on one of the festivals and my father coming home and singing all evening. This picture bore little resemblance to the careworn man I had left behind, but it cheered me a little to think that he had known happier days.

* * *

People have justly called the Nazis 'assassins of memory', and that is perhaps the most dire aspect of their destruction. The history of whole communities along with their members has been blotted out as though they had never existed. The shared reminiscences, the anecdotes about uncle this and cousin that are lost, never to be retrieved. Against this background I felt like an archaeologist garnering his pottery-shards. I was struggling to piece together some basis for a genuine sense of personal identity. Hitherto I had been a refugee brought up on the fringe of my foster parents' Polish-Jewish community, then later, the daughter-in-law inundated with the legends of her husband's family. Now, despite the sparseness of the material that was available to me, I was attempting to become a person in my own right.

It was not till thirty-five years after I left Vienna that I could bear to reverse that fateful journey. This time I made it by car. As we crossed into Germany from Belgium, I felt a shiver of horror. What would I find on the other side? I was surprised that the sun shone as brightly as it had done in Belgium and that people were going about their ordinary business in the streets. When I asked for directions from passers-by in my not-too-fluent German, they were polite and helpful. The past seemed more inexplicable than ever. We broke our journey and camped at Regensburg (the Ratisbon of the Browning poem) and then followed the bend of the Danube in an easterly direction. As we approached Vienna, I had a fit of panic and was for giving up the enterprise, but my husband encouraged me to go on till we reached a crowded camp-site on the western outskirts.

I had not expected to find my old home without difficulty. In my mind it was tucked away in some half-forgotten

Never-Never Land like Judy Garland's 'somewhere over the rainbow'. I was therefore astonished to find how easily I was directed to the district of Margareten where I had lived. We took a tram to the Ringstrasse where I recognised the spires of St. Stephen's Cathedral restored to their former dominance after being damaged in the war. We passed the opera house and the Parliament building with the figure of Athene, the goddess of wisdom, in front of it. Unbidden, a fellow-passenger, possibly hearing us talking in English, quipped: 'You notice she has her back to the building!'

I noticed, too, the word 'justice' on the motto above the portico!

I had to swallow hard as I approached the flats where I had lived. We got off the tram at the Margaretenstrasse and cut through to the Bräuhausgasse and there they were – unchanged – grey four-storey blocks with a courtyard in the middle. On the opposite side was the music school I had passed on the morning of the *Anschluss* and here were the stone steps I had often climbed on my way to our flat. I recognised the front door. As I walked along the landing, none of the names by the bell-pushes were familiar and I was too overcome to knock on any doors. Walking to the end of the road, I passed the post office, then the tiny children's playground quaintly named the *Hundsturm* and finally, the building where I had gone to school. This, I was told, was now occupied by the Red Cross.

When I went to the twentieth district where my aunt had lived, it was the same: the buildings were still there, but the people I had known were gone. I saw again the rose garden where I had wheeled my young cousins in their prams and the circular benches round the trees where I had sat watching the boats on the nearby Danube Canal. Later, while strolling in the Old City, I noticed a big stone chained to a wall. Into my mind flashed a memory of a walk I had taken with my father when he had pointed out a special stone to me. Incredulous, I rushed up to a passer-by and asked what the stone was.

'It's a relic of the Turkish siege of Vienna', he answered without hesitation.

It was the same stone!

Perhaps the most poignant moment of all was in Vienna's famous pleasure-ground, the Prater, where I had often been taken as a child. A little girl called out 'Papa!' and for a moment the years rolled back as I heard that word used again.

After this, there was little more to keep me in Vienna and I was glad to fold our tent and make for Italy.

On a later visit to Israel, my aunt told me that my father had been killed in Buchenwald. I could not bear to ask for more details, even assuming that she had any. When I went to Yad Vashem, the Holocaust memorial centre in Jerusalem, I learned that it might be possible to get information about my mother if I got in touch with the organisation for Jewish affairs in Vienna, the *Kultusgemeinde*. On my return to London, I rang them and gave them my mother's name, date of birth, etc. I waited with bated breath while they consulted their lists and gasped when they told me:

'Yes, we have some information about Paula Immerdauer.'

They gave me her last address in Vienna which was different from that of my aunt's flat in the Brigittenauerlande from which I had left, explaining that it was in a ghetto to which she had had to move. The last place for which they had a record of her was at Opole, on the Polish–Czech border, where there was some kind of internment camp.

* * *

By now I was quite well-informed about what had happened during the war in Europe. How and why were separate questions. I was increasingly aware of my distance in time and place from these events which I now felt strong enough to contemplate. I had seen *Shoa* and other filmed material about the Holocaust, but I had a growing feeling that I wanted to see where my parents had died and so to feel closer to them, however grim these places were bound to be. As most of my family had probably been killed at Auschwitz, I decided to go there to see it for myself. After some enquiries, I discovered that Polorbis, the official Polish tourist agency, runs a special six-day tour to places of Jewish interest, so in 1991 I joined a party of fifteen people who had booked to go on this tour. Some, like me, had come to mourn lost relatives, some to trace their roots in Poland and some out of historical interest. Half of our party were not Jewish.

Leaving Heathrow on a mild October morning, we flew to Warsaw and were immediately taken on a tour of the Jewish sites of the city. One of the main streets, originally called Jerusalem Street, had been renamed by the Nazis Adolf Hitler Street. It was now restored to its former name. Nearby was the original ghetto which occupied quite a large area of the city at first, but shrank as its inhabitants died of hunger or disease or were deported to the death camps. The site itself is now occupied by the featureless grey apartment-blocks built by the Communist regime after the ghetto was razed to the ground, but sections of the boundary wall have been preserved. We saw the memorial by Rapaport to the heroic fighters of the Uprising who, armed with only the most primitive weapons, kept the Nazi guns and tanks at bay for a whole month in a hopeless but courageous act of resistance. We stopped also at a place which the Nazis called *'Umschlagplatz'*. Here were the railway lines where people were put into closed wagons bound for Treblinka.

Next we saw the few traces of surviving Jewish life in Poland: the Yiddish Theatre and a small synagogue, now nicely restored, which had escaped destruction by the Nazis, as they had used it as a stable. We talked to some members of the congregation, mostly old men, and were told that the Jewish community of Warsaw, originally a third of the total population of the city, had shrunk to 900.

The next day was devoted to the trip to Cracow, and the following morning, to seeing the sights of the Old City. I had thought of Poland as a place of poor shanty-towns, but Cracow turned out to be as splendid as any great European city. We saw the royal palace, the university where Copernicus had

159

made his discoveries and the mediaeval cloth hall. We went inside the cathedral which houses the tombs of the Polish kings, and from the bell-tower, had a panoramic view of the city bisected by the river Vistula.

The fourth day of the tour was scheduled for the trip to Auschwitz. I was glad I was not going alone. After a one-and-a-half hour coach-ride from Cracow in the direction of Catowice, we were there. I braced myself to go through the infamous gates with their cynical slogan *'Arbeit macht frei'*, and past the fence, no longer electrified, with the notice *'Lebensgefahr'*, a warning obviously not intended for the prisoners.

Our guide, a pleasant-looking young Polish woman with an excellent command of English, told us what many of us already half-knew: that there were three camps there. Auschwitz One, which was the extermination camp where all but the fittest adults were selected for instant death, and Birkenau and Monowitz, which were labour camps. We saw the end of the railway line, and the ramp where people waited to be 'selected'. We were shown a film of Auschwitz as it was on the day it was liberated by the Russian Army. Then we walked round the compound, consisting of many blocks of identical low brick buildings. From outside they looked surprisingly sturdy and unthreatening, but inside they told another story. Some of the rooms had specimens of the filthy narrow palliasses on which two prisoners slept, and the wooden slatted bunks on which up to a dozen prisoners huddled under a single blanket in temperatures often well below zero. The starvation diet and long hours of heavy work made sure that few survived for long. As the trains of deportees rumbled across Europe, they could soon be replaced.

Finally we were taken to see the exhibits, already familiar from newspaper photographs: the mountain of children's shoes, the baby clothes, the piles of suitcases labelled with the victims' names, and the human hair bundled into sacks and woven into linings for the coats of German soldiers. One hut, we were told, had been piled high with valuables filched from the victims. Elsewhere in a glass case were hundreds of containers of the poison gas Zyklon B, and in another part, the ultimate obscenity – the only remaining gas chamber, with its oven made of strong cast iron and bearing the name of its manufacturer. The other gas chambers had been destroyed by the retreating Germans.

After a short memorial service, we turned to talk to our guide. She told us how upset she was when people asked her why the Poles were so anti-Semitic. She herself had no prejudice against Jews. I tried to explain to her the effect of the message of hate that for centuries has gone out from the Catholic Church and the refusal by some of their clerics even now to acknowledge that the Holocaust was principally, if not exclusively, a crime against the Jews.

'Yes, but some children were hidden in monasteries, and some Poles risked their lives to shelter Jews', she countered.

'And some were happy to betray them to the Nazis', I replied.

Ah well, one must not generalise too much. As if to confirm this, a party of local children led by their teacher and bearing flowers appeared. Would they learn about the destructive power of hatred from their visit? Another sight that lifted our spirits in that chilling place was a troop of Israeli teenagers there on a government-sponsored trip. They brandished their blue and white flags with the Star of David in the centre, not as a token of shame, but a symbol of pride. I wanted to touch their flag and shout some of the few words of Hebrew I know: *'Am Yisroel Chai!'* The Jewish people are alive!

Our route back to Warsaw took us near the monastry of Chestachowa. Some of our party were keen to see it and the coach driver agreed to stop there. We saw the splendidly ornate church and the picture of the Black Madonna which appears at four o'clock, heralded by a fanfare from a trumpet. After we left, I happened to glance idly out of the coach window. What I saw was a signpost which made me grip my husband's hand tightly.

It was to Opole!

Many years earlier, when I was studying for Higher School Certificate, I read some of the works of two of the giants of German *Kultur*: Goethe and Schiller. I knew that they were associated with Weimar, but whereabouts Weimar was I had no idea. I can still remember the pain and outrage I felt many decades later when, chancing to listen to a radio programme, I heard that the site of the notorious concentration camp of Buchenwald, where my father was killed, was close to Weimar. The place had previously not been easily accessible, as it was in the former East Germany. However, since travel to the former German Democratic Republic was now unrestricted, I decided to go there in the summer of 1992.

The German tourist office supplied an information-sheet which gave details of the sights of Weimar, and, surprisingly, included a page on Buchenwald. I had no difficulty in getting there by train from Paris after changing at the bigger town of Erfurt, which is on the route to Dresden and the Czech border.

In Weimar, walking downhill from the station towards the town-centre, you pass block after block of drab grey buildings. Then you come to a pleasant pedestrian precinct with elegant shops. This leads to a leafy square with a fountain at its centre and at the far side of the square is the *Goethehaus*. This is a plain, low-slung building covered in an attractive colourwash. Inside the house is a museum containing letters, manuscripts and some remarkably fine drawings done by Goethe during his visit to Italy.

The *Schillerhaus* has exhibits from his plays and models of contraptions for flying stage-entrances and exits. On a wall in the middle of the room are the words of the 'Ode to Joy'. A little further on is a page of the *Völkische Beobachter* newspaper dated 1935, showing Hitler and his swastika-emblazoned crew claiming the two poets as their heritage.

I asked one of the attendants about the curious juxtaposition of liberal philosophy and Nazism. Her answers were:

'That's a philosophical question. I was only a child at the time. So many innocent people suffered.'

She would be drawn no further on the subject.

After we had spent some days exploring the sights of Weimar, including the pleasant park by the river Ulm where Goethe had his summerhouse, we decided it was time to pay our visit to Buchenwald. The camp was situated on the Etterberg just above Weimar. You get there by bus from a stop near the railway station actually marked 'Buchenwald'! The bus takes you past some newish residential apartments and then, up and up on a road flanked by trees. I wondered about the unfortunates who had made that journey as prisoners, what they must have thought at each stage of this seemingly endless ascent. Eventually, the bus stopped at a memorial to the victims and then went on to the camp itself.

This occupied a vast area. The entrance gate is still there, but most of the huts are gone. There are enormous gravel walks like some nightmarish no-man's-land, punctuated by a few buildings. One of these houses a bookshop, another has been made into a museum, and a pointer indicates the crematorium. The museum shows the camp's history from its beginnings as a place of incarceration for political opponents of the Nazis. From the vantage-point of the hill you enjoy, ironically, a most beautiful view of Weimar. Here and there are memorials, mostly to Russian soldiers and Communists. There is one memorial to 600 Jews who were killed there after *Kristallnacht*. I felt that this was an incomplete and misleading picture of the scale of the atrocities against Jews. However, I dropped my bunch of flowers there, shed a few tears and prepared to leave.

I now noticed, to my surprise, that the camp site was thronged with visitors: families, student parties, groups of children. What, I wondered, had brought them there on a hot summer's day? I spoke to one family about this. The husband, startled by my interrogation, replied:

'Because it's part of our history. To make sure it doesn't happen again.'

When people ask me: 'Why do you want to go to those gloomy places?' my answer is the opposite of Chekov's 'Not knowing is better'.

For me there is strength in being in touch with reality, however grim. It is my particular sadness that there is no grave I can tend for my parents, though the flowers I dropped at Auschwitz and Buchenwald are a bow in that direction. I ask myself am I lucky to have been one of the ten thousand children who survived? I suppose if I had been given the choice, I would have opted for life. Nevertheless, when I look at nine-year-old children today, the thought of their being sent to a strange land with strange people and never seeing their relatives again fills me with horror. I know now that all of us who have had these experiences are deeply scarred by them.

As for the Germans, I used to think they had got off scot-free, judging by their confident bearing and noisy assertiveness in public places, but a wise German acquaintance tells me that this is a cover for insecurity. Sometimes I feel I would not mind swopping their insecurity for my loss, but on the whole, I would not care to have the albatross of their recent history round my neck.

Of course, the under-fifties have no personal guilt. Of the older generation, it seems that there was a small minority of heroic people who sheltered Jews at great danger to their own lives. They are remembered and honoured at Yad Vashem in Jerusalem by trees planted in their name. A larger minority enjoyed their task of torture and murder, while the majority went along with whatever was decreed, partly because they were indoctrinated to hate Jews, partly out of apathy, greed or fear. The same story was repeated in every European country under German occupation with the notable exception of Denmark, which would have no truck with Nazism and shipped its Jewish population to safety in Sweden.

The story is very mixed and defies generalisation. My friends in Cornwall owed their lives to a chance encounter with a clergyman of the Church of England in St. Paul's Cathedral who put up the money to sponsor them. Another woman told me 'I was saved by a French policeman and a Protestant pastor'.

One survivor tells how fellow-workers in a factory smuggled food to her, knowing she herself was being kept on starvation-rations; another describes how, on the long forced march from Auschwitz to Belsen, no one in the streets they passed gave them a crust of bread or a word of sympathy.

The lesson that needs to be learned from this period, which is now passing into history, is to tackle extremism before it gets too powerful, by all the civilised means at our disposal. A few years ago it would have been possible to be optimistic that the poison of anti-Semitism had lost its power. However, with the rise of the new nationalism and the denial by some academics that the Holocaust ever happened, there is no room for complacency.

11 · *Reunion*

So far I have kept strictly to the chronology of events in my life, but now I want to conclude by going back a few years to a phone call I received from a friend in the summer of 1988.

'Did you hear the "Woman's Hour" broadcast about the *Kindertransport*? Someone's organising a fifty-year reunion.'

I thanked her and rang the 'someone' who turned out to be Bertha Leverton, a small but energetic lady who was planning a mammoth event in June 1989, a reunion of the children who had been allowed to leave Germany, Austria and Czechoslovakia before the Second World War broke out. By a strange coincidence, the reunion was to take place exactly fifty years to the day after my arrival in England in June 1939.

So there we were, fifty years on, the oldest well into our sixties, and the youngest in their middle and late fifties. A thousand of us had answered the call and were queuing up at the Harrow Leisure Centre, waiting to take part in the celebrations. It took an hour for us all to get in and be issued with badges marked with our name, town of origin and the initials ROK (Reunion of Kindertransport) set in a boat-logo. As we filed in, some people exclaimed: 'It's just like our camp at Dovercourt!'

The Harrow Leisure Centre did indeed have the appearance of a giant holiday-chalet like the ones some of the children were housed in when they arrived. Some of the *Kinder*, like myself, had been privately fostered and therefore isolated from others with a similar experience; others had gone to hostels in places like Dovercourt, Brighton and Stoke Newington where they had led a communal life until sent out to work, in the case of the girls, and into the army, in the case of the boys.

166

Round the walls of the hall were blown-up pictures of children arriving at Harwich and Liverpool Street. A few were smiling bravely, many looked tired and bewildered and, most moving of all, one little girl was clutching a holdall in one hand and a doll in the other. Some people recognised themselves in the pictures. The body of the hall had tables labelled with the places of our origin, Berlin and Vienna being the most common. We sat down with people from the same town, trying to find some links. Most of us had parted from parents and siblings, never to see them again, but a lucky few had been reunited with their families later. The most emotional reunions were of people who had been in the same hostel and recognised each other despite grey hair and wrinkles. For me there was no such experience, but I enjoyed talking to people who had come here from the US, South America, Australia and Israel.

The proceedings began with a memorial service. Then there were speeches from the Home Office Minister whose predecessor had authorised the *Kindertransport*, and from Dame Simone Prendergast, whose mother had played a leading part in organising the operation which had enabled ten thousand of us to survive. One of the most interesting items in the programme was a question-and-answer session, when four of the *Kinder* answered questions from an invited group of teachers. A question about identity-problems elicited a vivid response, especially from those who had come over as very young children, knowing little about their real families. We ourselves learned a great deal from the stories of fellow-refugees: we had all had to contend with a new language and culture. Some of us had been kindly treated in foster homes, while others were exploited and expected to be grateful for the privilege of being alive.

The reunion ended on a cheerful note with a concert and singsong. We sang all the old favourites: the 'Lambeth Walk', 'We'll gather lilacs', 'Tipperary', and relived briefly the emotions of wartime: desperate optimism masking dark anxieties, and a tremulous hope for a better future.

It was good to participate in this and to remember that, despite the shadow of tragedy which can never quite leave us, this was indeed a celebration: we had all managed to make something of our lives, as teachers, librarians, entrepreneurs, scientists, mothers, fathers. Perhaps that is the most fitting tribute to our parents.